HANDBOOK OF WORLD DEVELOPMENT

The Guide to the Brandt Report

Compiled by GJW Government Relations with
Peter Stephenson

Foreword by Willy Brandt

Longman

Longman Group Limited
Longman House, Burnt Mill
Harlow, Essex CM20 2JE

Associated companies, branches and
representatives throughout the world

© G.J.W. Government Relations 1981

First published 1981

ISBN 0 582 64386 4

Printed in Great Britain by
Richard Clay (The Chaucer Press) Ltd,
Bungay, Suffolk

STX

Contents

Abbreviations

ACP	African, Caribbean and Pacific countries (Lomé Convention)
ADB	Asian Development Bank
AfDB	African Development Bank
CACM	Central American Common Market
CAP	Common Agricultural Policy (EEC)
CEAO	West African Economic Community
Comecon	Council for Mutual Economic Assistance
CW	Commonwealth
ECA	Economic Commission for Africa
GATT	General Agreement on Tariffs and Trade
GDP	Gross Domestic Product
GNP	Gross National Product
IADP	Inter-American Defence Board
IBRD	International Bank for Reconstruction and Development (World Bank)
IDA	International Development Association
IDB	Inter-American Development Board
IFPRI	International Food Policy Research Institute
ILO	International Labour Organization
IMF	International Monetary Fund
ISC	International Finance Corporation
N/A	Non-aligned
NIC	Newly Industrializing Country
OAPEC	Organization of Arab Petroleum Exporting Countries
OAS	Organization of American States
OAU	Organization of African Unity
OCAM	Afro-Malagasy and Mauritian Common Organization
ODECA	Organization of Central American States
OECD	Organization for Economic Co-operation and Development
OPEC	Organization of Petroleum Exporting Countries
UNCTAD	United Nations Conference on Trade and Development
UNESCO	United Nations Educational, Scientific, and Cultural Organization
UNIDO	United Nations Industrial Development Organization
WHO	World Health Organization

Foreword

Willy Brandt
Chairman   Independent Commission on International
Development Issues

Since the publication of *North–South : A Programme for Survival* there has been an increasing flow of reactions from various quarters. The draft bibliography already contains over 200 references which reflect the growing interest and the widening discussion in official and private circles.

The Report was aimed at two target groups in particular, the political leaders and the public at large. It was intended to break the deadlock of the negotiations between experts conducted at the numerous international meetings. It tries to focus attention on the importance of the North–South relationship in the context of the present international political and economic crisis, and it suggests a programme of immediate and long-term actions to improve these relations.

The public reaction has been positive, and there have been a large number of letters expressing agreement with the Report's analysis and general line of thinking. In many cases these reactions support the Commission's view but they also end up asking what the individual can do and how one can help to implement all the changes that obviously are necessary and cannot be avoided.

But it is also being said that the Report is too complex and too technical for many readers who would prefer to have some more accessible information on various points in order to gain a clearer understanding of the specific recommendations of the Report. The present guide provides such additional information and responds to the Commission's expectation expressed in my introduction to the Report (p.9–10):

> ... we hope to reach open-minded, responsible women
> and men all over the world. It is our ambition to enable
> ordinary people to see more clearly how their jobs and
> their daily lives are interlocked with those of communities
> at the other end of the world. We are asking them to think

things over, to be sensible and act humanely and thus help secure a common future.

Official reactions of governments and institutions follow the well-known pattern: they agree on many specific points but they argue that in various ways steps are being considered or progress has been made in principle while further study of specifics seems to be required. A typical example is the special session of the U.N. in August–September 1980 where a considerable number of statements contained references to the Report, some of them only indicating that the Report exists and cannot be neglected while others strongly supported its conclusions and called for implementation of its recommendations.

While there was a lot of general support and even a call to make the Report obligatory reading for all citizens of the world, no delegation to the special session expressed the view that the Report should serve as the only blueprint for the global negotiations.

A minority of individual critics took this line, however. They argued that the Report was unique in that it was the only programme of its kind, the only existing proposal on which a group of representatives of industrialized and developing countries had agreed and which – as a compromise among differing views – represented a package acceptable to all of them. Therefore, they say, it should be accepted as a stepping-stone and as a basis on which a deal should be possible to overcome the present international crisis. 'An act of leadership', it was called by Aurelio Peccei, and it was labelled 'the only game in town' by another reviewer.

In some countries parliaments discussed the Report and the debates continue. Changes in the mood of the public are affecting government positions, which in turn seem to be changing in response to the changes in overall economic trends.

Meanwhile the predicament of developing countries, and of the world economy in general, has deteriorated even more rapidly than the Report had foreseen, aggravated by the competing expenditure on armaments by East and West. The current crisis calls for bold responses to the problems that threaten all the world's people in order to produce a new climate for co-operation and to assist the global negotiations which now remain deadlocked in the United Nations.

The longer-term structural changes must not delay urgent action to face the crisis already at hand. The existing state of emergency in the world economy requires an immediate and direct response.

Rising unemployment, persistent monetary instability, exorbitant interest rates, insupportable payments deficits and unprecedented debts all point to the need for international negotiation. But many individual nations appear to be retreating into short-term national solutions which can worsen their own long-term prospects.

The Report highlighted four areas for emergency action:

1. A global food programme to stimulate world food production and to begin to abolish world hunger.
2. A global energy strategy to accommodate the need for security of both producers and consumers.
3. Additional financial flows to ensure the stability of national economies strained by precarious balance of payments, and mounting debts.
4. Reforms to achieve broader participation in international financial institutions and more balanced conditions for world trade.

Reforms in these areas could provide important benefits for both North and South, and taken together they point the way to breaking the existing deadlock and stimulating the world economy.

One of the important recommendations of the Report – that a North–South summit meeting should be organized in which a limited number of leaders should participate and agree on a new political initiative to break the deadlock in North–South negotiations – has been taken up and such a meeting is now scheduled for October 1981 at the invitation of the Austrian and the Mexican governments.

But, as the Report states:

> The shaping of our own common future is much too important to be left to governments and experts alone. Therefore, our appeal goes to youth, to women's and labour movements, to political, intellectual and religious leaders, to scientists and educators, to technicians and managers, to members of the rural and business communities. May they all try to understand and to conduct their affairs in the light of this new challenge.

I believe that the present publication will be a great help in the effort to promote a better understanding which is a precondition for appropriate action by individuals as much as for decision-making and action by governments.

Willy Brandt
June 1981

viii

Acknowledgements

We would like to thank David Grace for undertaking the research for the country entries, and Tembi Carter for her excellent typing.

Anthony Sampson, Peter Smith, Simon May and Peter Ayre gave invaluable editorial advice, and we would also like to thank the many people who assisted with essential information, encouragement and advice during the course of the work.

We are especially grateful to the Brandt Commission and the National Westminster Bank for their generous financial support which made the project possible.

Introduction

The Handbook of World Development contains two A–Z sequences: the first provides the key facts and explanations on the main issues considered by the Report of the Independent Commission on International Development Issues (the Brandt Report); while the second provides essential information about the 100 countries of the Third World that constitute Brandt's 'South'.

The subject entries consist of the themes and facts covered in the Brandt Report, and the actions that the Report urged, listed under headings in alphabetical order. Subjects cross-relate to each other; major themes may touch on a number of particular subjects, each with its own entry. So wherever in the course of an entry a subject is mentioned that has another entry to itself and is worth making a cross-reference to in the particular context, that subject is put into italics. For example, in the entry on Children, there are references to the entries on *UNICEF, Hunger and Malnutrition, Education, Literacy*, and *ILO*. But the aim has been for each entry to be capable of being read by itself, so where necessary particular matters are covered in more than one entry.

Most entries contain at least one quotation from the Brandt Report, and all quotations included are from there unless the contrary is stated or is obvious from the context. After each quotation a page reference is given. These refer to the English-language edition of the Brandt Report published by Pan Books Ltd, London, 1980, under the title **North-South: A Programme for Survival**. When the Report is referred to, we simply call it 'Brandt'.

Except in quotations, we always talk of 'North' and 'South', not 'developed' or 'developing' or 'Third World'. Although the Brandt Report itself employs all these usages, the 'South' as defined by Brandt is not quite the same as the category 'developing countries'. The most generally agreed list of such countries is that of the Development Assistance Committee of OECD. It includes all countries in Africa except South Africa, all in America except the United States and Canada, all in Asia except Japan, all in Oceania except Australia and New Zealand, *and* certain countries in Europe – Cyprus, Gibraltar, Greece, Malta, Portugal, Spain, Turkey and Yugoslavia.

The boundaries of Brandt's 'South', as shown in the Brandt Report, differ from the DAC's list in two respects: they include South Africa and they exclude the European countries in the DAC list except Turkey.

Other categories of countries referred to in development matters are the *Third World* (see entry later), which is not a precisely defined term but is usually used synonymously with Brandt's 'South'; and the poorer developing countries, called *Least Developed Countries – LLDCs* (see entry).

The country entries consist of the 100 countries defined as 'South' by the Brandt Report, excluding those with a population of less than half a million. Each entry outlines the geography and main economic indicators where available. All figures given in the country section of the book are taken from UN sources, with the exception of figures for GNP and defence expenditure. Figures for GNP are drawn from OECD Development Assistance Committee estimates (based on World Bank sources) for the year 1978, and growth rates are calculated for the period 1970–78. The defence expenditure figures are from the International Institute for Strategic Studies, London, and are for 1979–80. Where no expenditure figure is available, the information given (in brackets) is that of the number of men estimated to be in full-time armed service.

The abbreviation *bn.*, where used, signifies one thousand million.

A–Z Subject Entries

A—Z Subject Entries

Absorptive Capacity

The extent to which developing countries' resources of qualified people and other technical and managerial capabilities set a limit to the amount of aid and other investment they can handle is often called their 'absorptive capacity'. Brandt comments: 'some of the conditions of absorption have been created by the terms and conditions of present aid management, for example reliance on tied foreign exchange components of projects; far greater sums could be transformed into productive investment if they came in more freely usable forms. Greater *Technical Assistance* (especially if it is planned jointly with the recipients) could identify, prepare and implement projects in a way that would augment absorptive capacity'(87).

Access to Markets

'A key problem which has to be solved if long-term growth is to reach and stay at the higher levels is that of access to Northern markets for the South's manufactures'(69). In the post-1945 period there was a gradual relaxation of barriers through Multilateral Trade Negotiations under *GATT*, and for the South through the *Generalized System of Preferences*. But 'by the early 1960s exports of textiles and clothing from the Third World were already subject to voluntary export restraints'(177), which led to more restrictions in the North, especially in the form of *Non-Tariff Barriers* such as quotas. The *Multi-Fibre Arrangement* for clothing and textiles agreed that quotas for imports into the North should grow by at least 6 per cent a year, but this has not been totally fulfilled.

The political pressures for protectionism in the North, at a time of economic stagnation and growing unemployment, are obviously great. It is necessary to argue the point that protectionism also brings penalties, especially in encouraging inflation. 'A 1978 survey of all consumer goods in the USA except food and automobiles found that goods imported from Asia and Latin America were, on the average, sold for 16 per cent less than domestic products of the same quality'(178).

Brandt points out that 'in the past fears that imports from the South would cause significant unemployment in the North have proved to be wrong. A report of the EEC covering numerous studies of the effects in the United States, Germany, Britain, France and other countries leads to the opposite conclusion: the direct impact on jobs has been small compared to that of domestic technical progress, although pressure from increased imports tends to encourage productivity improvements'(176).

Although 'it is the *OECD* countries with their high purchasing power which will have to be the principal outlet for future expansion of export-oriented industrial production in the South', the *Comecon* countries could do more. 'They have a much lower proportion of manufactures in their imports from non-oil developing countries – about 15 per cent in 1976 – than the USA (about 40 per cent), Japan (24 per cent) or the EEC (about 29 per cent)'(175).

Added Value
The difference between the value of materials and the final price of the products made from them – the result of processing, manufacturing and marketing activities – is the 'added value' or 'value added'. In the development context, its particular significance is the added value between the price the South receives for its raw material exports and the final price of the manufactures made from them in the North. At present the South's share is low. A basic aim of the development process, especially of *Industrialization*, is to give the South a larger share of the world's total added value, even at such a mundane level as enabling the South to 'export sawn planks or furniture instead of logs, instant coffee instead of coffee beans, refined metals instead of ores'(42).

African Development Bank
see *Regional Development Banks*

African Transport and Communications Decade
A ministerial meeting of the *Economic Commission for Africa* (ECA), following the recognition at the Conference on International Economic Co-operation that Africa suffered particularly from a poor transport and communications infrastructure, hampering development, launched the African Transport and Communications Decade, 1978–88, supported by the UN. It is intended to 'harmonize, coordinate, modernize and develop communications of all kinds, including road, rail, water transport, telecommunications, radio, television and postal services'. The ECA programmes for 1980–83 call for $8 billion of expenditure, including $4 billion for roads and road transport.

Agrarian Reform

Disparities in land ownership, with a minority of landlords and large farmers owning half or more of the land, often mean that most of the rural population has only small patches of land, or occupies land as tenants or sharecroppers exploited by landlords, or works as *Landless Labourers*. This means that *Agricultural Development* often fails to benefit the rural poor, and is hampered also by the under-utilization of large estates. Agrarian reform to distribute land use more equally was recognized as a 'critical component' in agricultural development in the declaration of the *World Conference on Agrarian Reform and Rural Development*, 1979. The initial impact of reform is, however, often to disrupt production temporarily, and in any case poor farmers receiving land usually require initial financial help. International aid can help with these transitional problems.

Agricultural Development

'Agriculture provides 44 per cent of the poorest countries' GDP and 83 per cent of their employment. Yet they are not growing enough to feed their people'(80). *Food Aid* cannot be relied on to fill the gap. An increase in domestic *Food Production* must be the first priority of development.

'The poorer countries will need much additional help to increase their food output. Aid to agriculture in low-income countries was approximately $3 billion in 1977. Estimates by the *International Food Policy Research Institute (IFPRI)*, the *FAO* and the *World Bank* indicate needs for additional assistance to agriculture up to 1990 from $4 billion to over $8 billion a year, matched by very considerable additional investment and recurrent expenditure by the countries themselves'(93). But investment in food production in the South is in the long run more economical for the North than the cost of food aid.

Of the reasons for the 'food gap', 'the most fundamental difficulty is control and management of water'(81), whether there is too much (rains and floods damaging crops and leaching soils) or too little. *Irrigation* is a vital need, and is the biggest absorber of investment costs in agricultural development. 'Growing more food will also depend heavily on research, which can improve inputs of *Fertilizers* and seeds and result in more efficient methods of production'(81) as shown by the *Green Revolution*.

However, Brandt also stresses that 'new models are needed for agricultural development in the Third World. The western agricultural model with its high degree of mechanization and use of chemicals cannot be simply transferred to developing countries'(94). Farming systems must be developed that are appropriate to local circumstances and the ecological balance. Development must often be accompanied by *Agrarian Reform* of land tenure if it is to be effective and to alleviate rural poverty.

Aid

The expression 'Aid' is often used loosely to cover all forms of *Development Finance*, but it should more precisely, and more usefully, be restricted to mean Official Development Assistance – ODA. This is defined by the *Development Assistance Committee* of *OECD* as:

> 'grants or loans undertaken by the official sector, with promotion of economic development and welfare as main objectives, and at concessional financial terms (if a loan, at least 25 per cent 'grant element')'.

Technical co-operation is also included in aid – grants for training of nationals of developing countries and for teachers, advisers, etc., serving in those countries. Grants and loans for military purposes are not included. The 'grant element' in a loan is a measure, based on a Development Assistance Committee formula, of the extent to which the loan is concessional (a 'soft loan') compared to normal market terms. Aid may be 'tied', where purchases made with it must be from the donor country, or 'untied' where there is no such limitation.

'Aid' is therefore only part of the total of development finance, which includes private loans and investment flows. In recent years there have been heavy borrowings by the better-off countries of the South from commercial banks in the North, particularly as a consequence of the *Recycling of Funds* from the balance-of-payments surpluses of the richer *OPEC* countries. But for the poorest countries, 'aid' in the strict sense is their major source of funds for development.

The United Nations objective for development finance as a whole is 'one per cent of the GNP of developed countries for the net transfer of resources to developing countries, including private flows, and within it 0.7 per cent as a target for official development assistance'. The one per cent overall objective is being met, but only because of large private flows. Few countries have met the 0.7 per cent Aid target.

The principal aid givers of the North are the members of the Development Assistance Committee. The DAC's estimates of aid – Official Development Assistance – in 1979 as a percentage of the donor countries' GNPs range downwards from Sweden – 0.94 per cent; Netherlands – 0.93 per cent; Norway – 0.93 per cent; and Denmark 0.75 per cent (the only achievers of the 0.7 per cent target) through, e.g., France – 0.59 per cent; UK – 0.52 per cent; Germany – 0.44 per cent; to USA – 0.20 per cent; Austria – 0.19 per cent; Italy – 0.08 per cent.

Brandt notes that comparisons between countries' aid performances are not straightforward. There are ambiguities about what should be included, and 'some donors have argued that while their aid performance has been low, their trade policies are liberal'(225). But these points do not contradict the overall position, 'that the industrialized countries as a whole, and the major ones amongst them, have failed to fulfill expectations and commitments'(225). It is said that 'in many countries the political climate is at present unfavourable to an increase in aid ... but this climate must be changed. Citizens of such countries must be brought to understand that the problems of the world must be tackled too, and that a vigorous aid policy would in the end not be a burden but an investment in a healthier world economy as well as a safer world community ... that part of aid which will consist increasingly of grant-like flows to the poorest countries and regions cannot for the most part be claimed to bring to the donors economic rewards of quite the same extent as hard lending to better-off countries. It must be justified mainly on humanitarian grounds. But there is a broader interest in the North in providing such aid. We do not believe the world can live in peace or even that the North can prosper indefinitely if large sections of the South – with hundreds of millions of people – are shut out from any real prospect of progress and left on the margin of survival'(225). 'The achievement of goals with which we could be satisfied will require sums equal to more than a doubling of the current $20 billion of annual official development assistance'(273).

Algiers Action Programme

The 1973 Conference of Non-Aligned countries in Algiers adopted an Action Programme which introduced the term *New International Economic Order*, leading to the Declaration and Programme of Action agreed by the UN General Assembly in 1974, and the *Charter of Economic Rights and Duties of States*.

Alternative Energy Sources

The allied problems of *Oil Prices* and the eventual exhaustion of *Oil and Gas Production* can ultimately be solved only by the development of alternative non-exhaustible energy sources. But there are problems attached to all alternatives, 'of technology, of risk to the environment, and of costs'(166). Risk is particularly a problem with nuclear energy. In contrast, 'hydro-electric development is a well-known and feasible technology which must attract major new investment in the near future, particularly in the developing countries'(167). Solar energy would be particularly relevant to the needs of most Southern countries, and though more research is needed to make it generally competitive, it is already so for some land-locked countries. Brandt asks for 'the fruits of research on solar energy in the North to be made available on specially favourable terms to the poorer countries of the South'(167).

Anti-Poverty Strategy

Brandt places great emphasis on the need to ensure that development brings about the relief of *Poverty* – the poor must 'gain directly from growth and participate fully in the development process'(128). Overall economic development must be accompanied by policies 'to prevent the new economic power and wealth being concentrated in the hands of a small minority. In certain countries this may mean some sacrifice of quicker growth in favour of a broader but surer development which minimizes social strains; in others, research suggests, redistributive strategies may accelerate growth'(129).

Appropriate Technology

There is now an increased awareness that *Transfer of Technology* from the North may not result in the South receiving what is appropriate to its particular needs. Because there is a wider gap in countries of the South between standards in the advanced sectors of their economies and those in the rest 'perhaps the greatest technological problem facing developing countries is the essential need to upgrade technology in traditional agriculture and the *Informal Sector*' (131). This does not mean using technology outdated in the North, but 'appropriate technologies can include cheaper sources of energy; simpler farm equipment; techniques in building, services and manufacturing processes which save capital; smaller plants and scales of operation which can permit dispersal of activity ... an appropriate "consumption technology" can choose products which suit local income and objectives'(195). Appropriate Technology will therefore often take the form of what is sometimes called 'intermediate technology' specially designed for the needs of the South.

Brandt points out that this is one of the areas of *Mutual Interests* of North and South, in that much of the technology particularly appropriate to the present needs of the South may also become appropriate to the needs of a North that is having to cope with rising *Energy* costs.

Arab Aid Agencies
The rapid increase in balance of payments surpluses of most *OPEC* countries and the consequent *Re-cycling of Funds* has increased the importance of the Arab Aid Agencies in drawing on Middle East Funds to provide project aid and balance-of-payments support in the South. There are several multinational agencies as well as national ones. The Arab Fund for Economic and Social Development is limited to Arab countries and the Islamic Development Bank to Islamic ones; the Arab Bank for Economic Development in Africa is one of the agencies with a wider scope. Commitments made by the Arab Aid Agencies in 1978 totalled only $310·9m.

Arab Fund for Economic and Social Development
see *Arab Aid Agencies* and *Regional Development Banks*

Arms Spending
Brandt points out the depressing fact that 'the world's military spending dwarfs any spending on development. Total military expenditures are approaching $450 billion a year, of which over half is spent by the Soviet Union and the United States, while annual spending on official development *Aid* is only $20 billion. If only a fraction of the money, manpower and research presently devoted to military uses were diverted to development, the future prospects of the Third World would look entirely different'(117).

Some of this wasteful spending is by countries of the South, often encouraged by the North. Sales of weapons by the North to the South are increasing. Although some countries of the South are becoming significant arms exporters, about 70 per cent of arms exports to the South come from the USA and USSR, with France, the UK and Italy being the other leading suppliers. 'With the recession in the arms industry in the early

1970s ... the drive to sell weapons to the Third World was intensified, often aimed at stimulating new demand irrespective of real defence needs. These military-industrial pressures in the North are often reinforced by and connected with contacts in the developing countries, many of whom have military governments or strong military élites who want to be equipped with modern weaponry to enhance their prestige. Arms exports by Eastern Europe too have been influenced by the availability of surplus weapons and the need to earn foreign currency'(120). In 1978 talks between the USA and USSR about limits on the transfer of conventional weapons to the South broke down: Brandt hopes further efforts will be made.

On proposals for a special tax on arms trade, Brandt notes the objection that this would in some sense 'legitimize' arms expenditures, but nevertheless believes that 'military expenditures and arms exports might be one element entering into a new principle of assessment for international taxation' (123) to provide *Automatic Revenues* for development.

Asian Development Bank
see *Regional Development Banks*

Automatic Revenues
There have been various proposals for methods of international taxation that could be used to raise money for development *Aid* on an automatic basis. Brandt supports the concept – 'at present the amount of aid depends on the uncertain political will of the countries giving it, and is subject to the shifting priorities of annual appropriations and the vagaries of legislatures. With more assured forms and methods developing countries could plan on a more predictable basis, making aid more effective'(244). This would not mean that aid was allocated automatically to particular countries: it would be channelled through international agencies.

Possible taxes that Brandt believes should be considered include 'placing a levy on international trade, on arms trade, on international investment, on hydrocarbons and exhaustible minerals, on durable luxury goods, on military spending [see *Arms Spending*], on the consumption of energy, on internationally traded crude oil, on international air travel and freight transport, or on the use of the "international commons" – ocean fishing, offshore oil and gas, sea-bed mining, the use of space orbits, radio and telecommunication frequencies and channels. The yield would vary widely, from about $250 million from a one per cent levy on international passenger and freight transport, to about $7 billion from a 0.5 per cent levy on international trade'(244).

Is there any real hope of nations accepting such an approach? Brandt replies 'those who argue that the concept of international taxation is unrealistic in the light of public opinion should recall that the same was said about national income tax in nearly all western countries a century ago'(247).

Bretton Woods
The 1944 conference which founded the *IMF* and the *World Bank* was held at Bretton Woods in New Hampshire, USA. These institutions and their affiliates are therefore sometimes referred to as the 'Bretton Woods organizations'.

Caribbean Development Bank
see *Regional Development Banks*

Cash Crops
One obstacle to improvement of food supplies in the South is that *Transnational Corporations* often develop cash crops for export at the expense of local food availability (96). This was one of the problems examined at the *World Conference on Agrarian Reform and Rural Development*, 1979.

Central American Bank for Economic Integration
see *Regional Development Banks*

Charter of Economic Rights and Duties of States
In 1972 *UNCTAD* established a Working Group to draw up a draft charter of economic rights and duties of states. The final version was adopted by the General Assembly in December 1974, developing themes in the Declaration on a *New International Economic Order* agreed earlier that year.

It covers such matters as national sovereignty over wealth, natural resources and economic activities, including non-intervention by *Transnational Corporations* in host states' internal affairs; free and non-discriminatory development of international trade; international co-operation in structural changes to the world economy for more rational and equitable international economic and social relations; promoting the *Transfer of Technology*; grant by developed countries of generalized preferential economic treatment to developing countries; *Economic Co-operation Between Developing*

Countries; enhancement of the role of developing countries in invisible trade; just and equitable *Terms of Trade* for developing countries; equitable sharing of the benefits of *Ocean Exploitation*; and international co-operation in preservation of the environment.

Children
Childhood in the South is rarely easy and is often a battle against deadly adversity. For many it ends when it has scarcely begun. 1979 was the *International Year of the Child*. *UNICEF* estimates that of the 122 million children born in that year, one in ten was dead by the beginning of 1981. Brandt says 'there are still countries in Africa where one child in four does not survive until its first birthday'. Living leads to more suffering. 'In some low-income countries studies have shown as many as 40 per cent of pre-school children exhibiting clinical signs of malnutrition'(90). In 1978 more than 12 million children under the age of five died of *Hunger*. Malnutrition can cause permanent harm: of the estimated 140 million disabled children in the world, three-quarters live in the South. Protein deficiency affects 100 million children under five.

Though *Education* in the South is improving, with rising *Literacy*, 'in poor families there is often a conflict between the need of the young for education and the need for the family as a whole to enlist children as supplementary producers or earners of income. A report on child labour in the Third World, produced by the *ILO* in 1979, gave shocking evidence of the numbers of children working long hours for negligible wages'(58).

Comecon
see *Eastern Europe*

Commodities
Despite progress in *Industrialization*, the South is still heavily dependent on the production and export of commodities, and the North is heavily dependent on the South as a source of supply. Quite apart from oil, some countries of the South 'obtain almost all their export earnings from one commodity; for example, Zambia (94 per cent from copper), Mauritius (90 per cent from sugar), Cuba (84 per cent from sugar) and Gambia (85 per cent from groundnuts). In 1970–72 over half the non-oil developing countries obtained more than 50 per cent

of their export earnings from one or two crops or *Minerals*' (145). Meanwhile, as far as the interests of the North are concerned, '60 per cent of world exports of the major agricultural and mineral commodities other than oil originate from the Third World' and 'in future the industrialized countries both in the West and in the East are likely to become more dependent on importing minerals and raw materials from developing countries'(148).

Brandt's proposals on commodities are 'of two main kinds: those which relate to the development of processing and marketing in the producing countries, and those which relate to price and earnings stabilization'.

The first kind of proposals are basically concerned with obtaining for the South a bigger share of the *Added Value* in products derived from commodities. This is part of the general need for more *Industrialization* and is therefore an integral aspect of the whole development process.

Most of the international involvement in commodity matters is concerned with Brandt's second category, prices and earnings. Prices of commodities, especially of agricultural products, are liable to fluctuate because of variations in production due to natural causes. But this can then be exacerbated by the effect of trade cycles, which have a multiplied effect on the producing countries because stock changes cause demand for the commodities to go up and down more than the underlying economic trends – hence the importance of stock measures in international action on commodities. And 'in some situations the activities of middlemen tend to result in heightened price fluctuation at the producer level'(46).

Brandt quotes Zambia as an example of the effect of price fluctuations combined with dependence on one product. The fall in copper prices meant that 'the volume of imports Zambia could buy fell by 45 per cent between 1974 and 1975 and the GDP fell by 15 per cent'(145). By comparison, the 1974 'oil shock' for the industrialized countries, with all its major consequences, in fact represented a cost to their GNP of only 2.5 per cent.

There has also been concern in the South that the *Terms of Trade* might be tending to move permanently against them, with commodity prices rising more slowly than the prices of the manufactures they import. Brandt believes that this is not in fact a problem in the long-term, and that the South's need is for price stabilization rather than 'any attempt to maintain artificially high prices'(147).

Brandt argues strongly that North and South have important *Mutual Interests* in commodity price stabilization. The North needs security of supply, which is endangered if price fluctuations discourage investment now for future production. There is also the problem of *Inflation* in the industrialized countries, which can be made worse by unstabilized commodity prices. But price stabilization is not easy. 'Consumers lose interest in stabilization when prices are declining and producers lose interest when they are rising ... agreement between producing and consuming countries on the price range to be defended has always been difficult'(149).

UNCTAD IV in 1976 adopted an Integrated Programme for Commodities, to comprise a *Common Fund* and *International Commodity Agreements* (ICAs) on more commodities of export importance to the South than are covered at present. The Common Fund would have two 'Windows'. The First Window would finance buffer stocks and the Second Window would finance other investments which could help the production, processing and marketing of the South's commodities. Agreement on the elements of the Common Fund was reached in March 1979; implementation is still being negotiated.

Brandt says that the work of the Common Fund and the ICAs cannot be expected to 'succeed in removing all export income fluctuations'(153). There is a large role still to be played by such export earnings stabilization schemes as the *Compensatory Financing Facility* of the *IMF* and the *Stabex* scheme of the European Community.

Common Fund

The *UNCTAD* IV agreement on an Integrated Programme for Commodities envisaged that it would be based on two elements: a Common Fund to finance certain activities concerned with *Commodities*, and *International Commodity Agreements* on prices and marketing, financed by the Common Fund.

The fund is to have two 'Windows'. The First Window would finance buffer stocks, and the Second Window would finance other investments that could help the production, processing and marketing of commodities. An agreement reached in March 1979 on the principal elements of the Common Fund differs from the original scheme mainly over financing. There is now to be an initial paid-up capital of $400 million for stocking operations. In addition, 'the Fund will also receive cash deposits from International Commodity Agreements associated with it, equivalent to one-third of their maximum capital requirements. On the assumption that $6 billion of capital resources will eventually be required for the Common Fund these cash deposits would provide a further $2 million'(150). So most of the Fund's resources would come only from Fund members participating in the particular commodity agreements concerned.

Common Market
see *European Community* and *Free Trade Areas and Common Markets*

Compensatory Financing Facility
As one of the special facilities of the *IMF – International Monetary Fund*, this provides member countries with loans to help them to cope with the effects of problems not of their own making, principally unexpected falls in export earnings. Brandt argues that the terms should be more generous, without the quota limits that apply to ordinary IMF loans, and that account should also be taken of movements in import prices 'as the rationale for balance of payments lending is in fact to forestall the need for harmful cutbacks in the flow of imports that may otherwise adversely affect development plans'(217).

'If quota limits are removed, if the coverage is enlarged to include food import requirements or other major causes of deficits beyond the country's control, if shortfalls are measured in real terms and if repayments are more flexible, the Compensatory Financing Facility might require much greater funding, which we estimate at about $12 billion, three times its present size'(218).

Comprehensive New Programme of Action for the Least Developed Countries
This was adopted at the 1979 meeting of UNCTAD, covering matters of *Aid* and trade.

Consultative Group for International Agricultural Research
This Consultative Group is sponsored by the *World Bank*, *UN Development Programme* and the *FAO*, with funds from national governments and development institutions. It has set up nine international agricultural research institutes, to carry out research concerned with specific food crops, the development of appropriate farming systems, or livestock problems.

Corruption
Brandt believes that there should be frank North–South discussion of the problems of 'waste and corruption, oppression and violence ... to be found in many parts of the world'(10). Although some transnational corporations have engaged in 'unethical political and commercial activities ... in some cases governments may be as much to blame as the corporations and the distinction between bribery and extortion can be a fine one'(189). Brandt stresses, however, that 'the work for a new international order cannot wait until these and other evils have been overcome'(10).

Death Rates
See *Life Expectancy*

Debt-servicing Burden
The result of the major *Recycling of Funds* that took place during the 1970s has been that 'loans in the international private market now account for nearly 40 per cent of the outstanding debt of developing countries compared to only 17 per cent in 1970'(222). In consequence of this growth, added to the repayment needs of public development finance (all very much increased because of the impact of *Oil Prices* on balances of payments), the countries concerned now face heavy debt-servicing burdens. 'In the three-year period 1979–1981 the aggregate payments for servicing the debts of all developing countries excluding *OPEC* are estimated at $120 billion ... the borrowing needs of these countries are likely to rise considerably further into the 1980s. As the loans fall due, they need to borrow more in order to repay and service them'(223). There are now fears that defaults on payments, which have not yet been a problem, may develop and cause a crisis in the international financial system. Brandt concludes that there must be new sources of long-term finance for the South.

Decade for Drinking Water and Sanitation
The 1980s were designated this decade by the 1977 UN Water Conference, for improvement of safe *Water Supplies and Sanitation* in the South.

Deforestation
Forests cover one-fifth of the world's land surface. They are important for the Third World, particularly in preventing soil erosion and in providing *Firewood*; and for the whole world in

absorbing the excess carbon dioxide produced by burning fossil fuels – which otherwise could raise atmospheric temperatures with disastrous effects on climates. The extent to which forests are disappearing without being replaced (11 million hectares a year in the Third World) 'would halve the stock of usable wood by the end of this century'(20) and threaten all these functions. Shrinking of the Amazon forest is causing particular worry about carbon dioxide absorption.

Development Assistance Committee (DAC)
The DAC is a committee of *OECD* – the Organization for Economic Co-operation and Development.

Development Finance
'The developing countries obtain finance from a number of sources: government-to-government aid programmes and export credit agencies; international financial institutions, including the *World Bank* Group and *Regional Development Banks*, the *IMF*, the UN agencies and other multilateral funds; private investment, much of it by multilateral corporations (see *Transnational Corporations*); and commercial banks. The creation and expansion of the system of financing development in recent decades amounts to a major change in international economic co-operation'(221).

'A very big change has occurred in the composition of the total flows to the developing countries. In 1960, 60 per cent came from concessional *Aid* or Official Development Assistance. By 1977, more than two-thirds was commercial, mainly from private bank loans, direct investment and export credits'(222). One result is a heavy and increasing *Debt Servicing Burden* on the South.

Brandt examines needs for development finance firstly in terms of the types of countries.

'The low-income countries, which contain most of the world's poor people, have a very limited capacity to participate in the world economy ... they need massive investments in irrigation and agriculture to avoid dangerous food deficits towards the end of the decade; and large outlays for improving *Health*, nutrition and *Literacy* ... Existing assistance to the poorer countries is inadequate ... the aggregate needs of all the Least Developed Countries for external capital are estimated by *UNCTAD* at $11 billion annually during the 1980s and $21 billion during the 1990s, to support a 6.5 per cent rate of GDP growth (3.5 per cent per capita)'(228).

For the whole group consisting of least developed, low-income and lower-middle-income countries (all below $520 income per head), the need will be 'annual aid in the 1980s in the range of $40–54 billion (in 1980 dollars) either for achieving a 3.5 to 4 per cent growth in per capita income, or for obtaining resources equal to half the costs of meeting essential human needs, the other half being borne by the countries themselves'(228).

The middle-income and higher-income developing countries 'need development loans on terms and in forms which suit their stage of development. Their total borrowing requirements will be affected by the growth and openness of the markets for their exports'(229). The World Bank projection, assuming 7.2 per cent annual inflation, is of $155 billion 'borrowing by these countries from commercial banks and other private sources'(229) in 1985 and $270 million by 1990, compared to less than $40 billion annually in 1975–77.

In sector terms, *Food Production* development in low-income countries will need an additional $8.5 billion of aid annually in the 1980s. 'The Lima target for *Industrialization* in the Third World . . . would need a total annual investment of $40–60 billion between 1980 and 1990, and $120–140 billion between 1990 and 2000 . . . if foreign financing is to meet fully the foreign exchange component of the projects, industry in the Third World would need $25–35 billion from abroad annually over the next decade'(230) compared to about $10 billion now. For *Energy* and *Minerals*, 'oil, gas, coal and minerals between them will need external finance of at least $6.5 billion per annum, plus finance for renewable sources of energy which are so far unquantified but still vital for the future'(231).

One particular difficulty in development finance is that of *Programme Lending* v. *Project Lending* – the fact that it is easier to obtain finance for particular development projects than overall finance for development programmes. The manufactures-exporting countries in the South tend to be short of *Export Finance*, especially for capital goods. More financial support is needed for the encouragement of *Economic Co-operation Between Developing Countries*. And there is special need for more finance for effective *Commodities* price stabilization.

All these needs will not be met by the present scale and approaches of development finance. Brandt urges that the work of the *IMF* and the *World Bank* should be complemented by a new institution 'which might be called a *World Development Fund*'(252) to cover the gaps identified. But meanwhile an action programme is required to substitute more direct lending for the *Recycling of Funds* that has taken place through the commercial banking system, including 'special benefits, with subsidized interest and extended maturities, to the poorest countries'(254). Immediate action through international agencies should include 'effective utilization of the increased borrowing capacity of the *World Bank* resulting from the recent decision to double its capital to $80 billion, and doubling the borrowing-to-capital ratio of the World Bank from its present gearing of 1.1 to 2.1, and similar action by *Regional Development Banks*; the use of *IMF* gold reserves either for further sales, whose profits would subsidize interest on development lending, or as collateral to borrow for on-lending to developing countries'(255). All this adds up to a need for what Brandt calls 'massive transfers' of funds to the South, on a much greater scale than present development assistance.

Diseases

'Most people in the *Poverty Belts* suffer from a combination of long-standing malnutrition and parasitic diseases'(82). These diseases hamper rural development by lowering people's productivity. About one billion people are at risk from malaria, bilharzia affects 180–200 million, sleeping sickness affects 35 million and river-blindness in Africa affects 20 million. Control and eradication of such diseases has been shown to be favourable to development, through physical and psychological impacts.

Disease control requires chemical compounds and drugs which are very expensive in relation to poverty-belt incomes. Brandt recommends more *WHO* spending on research into disease control – about $560 million – and about $2.5 billion of development aid on disease control over the next twenty years.

Earnings Stabilization Schemes
see *Commodities* and *Compensatory Financing Facility*

East African Development Bank
see *Regional Development Banks*

Eastern Europe

In the earlier post-colonial period, the countries of the South accepted the argument by the Soviet Union and other East European countries that they were not responsible for the 'colonial heritage'. More recently, as the international economic links from Eastern Europe have developed, there have been demands from the South for these countries to play what the 1979 meeting of the Group of 77 called 'an increasingly more active role' in development aid and trade for the South. The Eastern European trade and monetary alliance, Comecon (Council for Mutual Economic Assistance) has the Mongolian People's Republic, Cuba and Vietnam as members from the South.

Ecology

One of the major *Environment* threats is in those countries of the *Poverty Belts* who 'exist in a fragile tropical environment which has been upset by the growing pressure of people'(79). These pressures, causing *Deforestation* and desertification may result in 'irreversible destruction of their ecological systems'(47). Brandt stresses the need for long-term measures in these countries, on water and soil management, reforestation, etc., with guaranteed aid from which the return could come only slowly. Some of these matters were covered in the *Comprehensive New Programme of Action for the Least Developed Countries*, 1979.

Economic and Social Commission for Asia and the Pacific

Set up by the UN in 1947 as the Economic Commission for Asia and the Far East. Changed to present name in 1974. Its headquarters are in Bangkok, with activities including general development research and advice, and the establishment of regional centres for training and research.

Economic Commission for Africa

Set up by the UN in 1958, with headquarters in Addis Ababa, to carry out research and provide advice on economic and technological development in Africa. Initiated the *African Transport and Communications Decade*.

Economic Commission for Latin America
Set up by the UN in 1948, with headquarters in Santiago, to carry out research and provide advice on economic development in Latin America, in conjunction with the Latin American Institute for Economic and Social Planning, established in 1962.

Economic Co-operation Between Developing Countries
At the 1977 Ministerial Meeting of the *Group of 77*, there was agreement on a 'short-term action plan for global priorities in Economic Co-operation Between Developing Countries',particularly in the form of more *Regional Co-operation and Integration*.

Economic Development Institute
Established by the World Bank in 1955, originally to provide mid-career training in economic management techniques for senior officials from developing countries, it now has the broader scope of covering problems and methods of identifying, preparing, appraising, executing and managing development projects.

Education
In most of the South, spending on education has grown faster than population in the last two decades, and *Literacy* has improved. Secondary education is expanding, but is still low: 'in only one-third of Asian countries and in two-fifths of Latin American countries'(57) were more than 40 per cent of the age-group in secondary school. Education for girls is still relatively limited; they tend to form less than 40 per cent of primary school enrolment. Brandt notes that 'education ramifies into the economy, politics and society reflecting inequalities and entrenched interests'(58). In particular, 'higher education has often expanded too fast in relation to many countries' ability to employ graduates ... are schools and universities teaching the right subjects to the right people?'(58).

Energy
The future availability and cost of energy is the chief matter of concern to the world economy. The quadrupling of oil prices by *OPEC* in 1973–74 had dramatic economic consequences. But it did make oil prices reflect the reality of the relationship

between future demand and likely future supply as they had not done before. There is general agreement that one result must be a major effort to develop *Alternative Energy Sources*. The 1981 UN Conference on New and Renewable Sources of Energy will be examining what can be done. But for at least the next two decades 'oil will remain the lifeblood of industrial society'(161).

A particular significance of the oil problem in North–South relations is that 'the use of energy in the world is grossly unbalanced ... one American uses as much commercial energy as two Germans, nine Mexicans, 19 Malaysians, 53 Indians or 438 Malians ... 85 per cent of the world's oil consumption takes place in the industrialized world'(162). This disproportion is a reflection of the South's low economic standards. And as the South develops, whatever energy conservation measures are introduced, energy consumption there must grow. So the burden of world energy conservation measures must be borne by the North.

Since the 1973–74 crisis it is in fact the countries of the South which have tended to find the most difficulty with energy supply. At the same time, they are least able to bear the higher energy costs. In discussions for an international energy strategy, notably those at the Conference on International Economic Co-operation in 1975–77, the countries of OPEC and those of the rest of the South have combined in insisting that the energy price and supply question 'was only part of the broader problem of restructuring the world economy'. Special measures by OPEC to protect the poorer oil-importing countries have been found difficult because of lack of refineries in those countries: there are proposals for these to be built jointly by oil-exporters and by OPEC countries who could then guarantee them security of supply. At the same time, increased financial aid is needed for them to meet higher energy costs.

Environment
Preservation of the world environment is one of the obvious *Mutual Interests* of North and South. 'Few threats to peace and the survival of the human community are greater than those posed by the prospects of cumulative and irreversible degradation of the biosphere on which human life depends'(115). The problems involved were described at the UN Conference on the Human Environment in 1972.

Part of the threat to the environment comes from industrial

pollution, and the South's need for industrial expansion can lead it too readily to accept adverse environmental effects. The other part is the ecological threat from the pressure of *Population Growth*, causing much of the *Deforestation* and desertification. Development activities need to be accompanied by an 'environmental impact assessment'.

The difficulty of international action to preserve the 'global commons – especially the oceans, the atmosphere and outer space'(115), is shown by the slow progress of the UN *Law of the Sea Conference* towards the hoped-for international *Seabed Authority*. Countries of the North are meanwhile going ahead with purely national plans for sea-bed mineral recovery and other forms of *Ocean Exploitation*.

European Community

The principal aid and development policies of the European Community as a unit (to which must be added the national policies of the 10 member states) are carried out through the Lomé Agreement. The current agreement, Lomé II, is a five-year one from 1980, its predecessor having run from 1975. The agreement is with 60 'ACP' countries – African, Caribbean and Pacific, mostly former colonies of EEC members. It includes trade co-operation, with benefits from the *Generalized System of Preferences*, the *Stabex* system of export earnings support for certain *Commodities*, an agreement on guaranteed imports of sugar, grants from the European Development Fund (1980–85 budget, $3000m.) and loans from the European Investment Bank. The Community also gives food aid to needy countries of the South generally, not just ACP countries. The 1981 programme will be worth about $700m. There is, however, criticism in the South about the effects on world food markets of subsidized food exports under the Common Agricultural Policy (CAP) and continued CAP protection against imports of some food products from the South into the European Community.

Exchange Rates

The fluctuations in currency exchange rates since the early 1970s, when most currencies began to float in value against each other, has caused difficulty for everyone including the countries of the South. 'While some developing countries have floating or "crawling" exchange rates, most are pegged to major currencies, or to a basket of currencies, because their own money markets are very rudimentary and their economies are vulnerable. The floating of the major currencies introduces uncertainties about real earnings from exports and real costs of imports since exports and imports are often involved in currencies which move against each other in unpredictable ways. This kind of uncertainty discourages allocation of resources to producing goods for export or for competition with imports, and introduces complications in external debt management'(207).

Brandt's proposals for dealing with this problem are part of the recommendations for reform of the *International Monetary System*.

Export Finance

Exports of capital goods are often dependent on long-term credit being given to customers. Such exports are becoming increasingly important for some developing countries. Their own needs for *Development Finance* make it more difficult for them than for the Northern nations to provide this credit, in the way, for example, that the Export Credit Guarantee Department (ECGD) helps UK exporters. Brandt points to a need (234) which is at present specifically met only for Latin America, through the Inter-American Development Bank and the Latin American Export Credit Bank.

Fair Labour Standards

Trade unions in the North 'raise questions when they suspect that wages in developing countries are being held down by exploitation of a weak and unorganized labour force, by excessive working hours or by the use of child labour'(182), especially if this produces excessive profits, sometimes for *Transnational Companies* who are the unionists' own employers in the North. The World Employment Conference in 1976 declared 'the competitiveness of new imports from developing countries should not be achieved to the detriment of fair labour standards' and in 1978 the International Confederation of Free Trade Unions demanded the insertion of a 'social clause' in trade agreements to control labour standards in exporting countries.

FAO – Food and Agriculture Organization

One of the original UN specialized agencies, founded in 1945, to increase the efficiency of the production and distribution of all food and agricultural products, to improve the condition of rural populations and to raise levels of nutrition in developing countries. Headquarters are in Rome. 1980–81 budget is $279m.

Fertilizers
Brandt does not expect a problem of fertilizer *supply* to result from oil shortage, even though 'modern farming is heavily dependent on oil-based nitrogenous fertilizers'. At present, they only take 2 or 3 per cent of oil production. In the long term 'there could be alternative sources of nitrogen from coal or from the biological fixation of nitrogen in the soil'(100) and other sources.

The fertilizer *price* problem is more serious. 'It is particularly important to guarantee fertilizer supplies at reasonable prices to low-income countries'(100). In 1974 the *FAO* established the International Fertilizer Supply Scheme with fertilizer-producing countries and the international fertilizer industry to make fertilizer available at set prices to such countries.

Financial Food Facility
see *Food Stocks*

Firewood
'In most of the countries in the poverty belts, nine-tenths of the people depend on firewood as their chief source of fuel'(83). The pressure of *Population Growth* leads to more demand for firewood, which accentuates *Deforestation*, with consequential damage to *Ecology* and *Food Production*. An indirect effect of firewood shortage is that more animal manure is used for fuel instead of fertilizer with further ecological impact. Brandt urges more effort for reforestation with fast-growing tree varieties which can be used for firewood inside a decade.

Fish
'Most developing countries remain considerably below the average world intake of fish protein per capita'(96). The *FAO* has given particular attention to the development of large-scale fishing in the South in the 200-mile 'Exclusive Economic Zones' newly defined in the draft *Law of the Sea*: at present 'ocean fishing is largely in the hands of developed

countries'(97). Eight regional fishing committees work to improve technical resources and marketing facilities in the South. As well, international action to conserve ocean fish stocks is an aspect of the general need for international control of *Ocean Exploitation*. Fishing in the South is one of the activities that has suffered from shortages of oil supplies in recent years.

Food Aid

Brandt maintains that although food aid 'has been criticised in the past, whether for its political exploitation or for the disruption of agricultural incentives in recipient countries ... it need not be a disincentive to agricultural production provided that effective demand for food is raised to clear the market at a price which rewards domestic producers'(101).

Food aid requirements should be calculated not just according to expected deficits, but 'also related to programmes for increasing investment in agriculture'(102). Often up to 60 per cent of the funds needed for such agricultural investment as irrigation work is required for the construction workers' food. Food aid here is a direct input to investment, to be phased out as the investment results in higher food production.

However, continuity of food aid, critical anyway, becomes even more vital if it is to be part of investment. The 1975 *World Food Conference* target of 10 million tonnes of cereals aid in a year has not yet been reached. Food aid other than cereals is also needed. Renewal of the Food Aid Convention is 'a matter of urgency'. Meanwhile, ability to cope with food emergencies must be improved by better *Food Stocks*.

Food Stocks

To ensure secure supplies of food, in the face of 'major swings in grain production every few years'(99), better international arrangements for food stocks are needed. Negotiations for a new International Grains Agreement opened early in 1978, to include a Coarse Grains Convention and Wheat Trade Convention. The North countries disagreed with the South's scheme for the creation of a fund to be managed within the Arrangement, to finance the construction of storage facilities, the purchase of grain and the costs of running the reserves. 'It is estimated that developing countries would need to hold 5–7 million tonnes of a 20–30 million tonnes reserve; the acquisition and storage construction costs involved have been put at roughly $1.75 billion'(99). The negotiations were adjourned *sine die* in February 1979.

In addition, the UN General Assembly in 1975 urged an international emergency food reserve of 500 000 tonnes of cereals. Contributions by late 1979 were only 350 000 tonnes; meanwhile, it is thought 750 000 tonnes would be needed for 1981.

All this would still leave problems for countries with fluctuating food import needs, and a 'financial food facility' has been advocated to help 'low income countries in times of domestic production shortfalls or unexpectedly abrupt increases of the price of food imports'. Brandt supports this concept (100).

Food Trade
Policies for control of food imports and exports, and subsidizing of exports, pursued by countries of the North to protect and support their own farmers, damage the South. Even subsidies on exported surpluses from the North, which help some countries of the South, compete with exports from others. 'These policies have accentuated world grain price fluctuations'(100). Because, when production is low and prices are high, the consumers of the North do not consume much less, the poorer countries bear the brunt. If there were freer trade in foodstuffs, 'both within and between North and South'(100) these impacts would be lessened. Improved food processing and marketing capability in the *Least Developed Countries* is particularly needed, to encourage food trade and make more effective use of local production.

Food Production
'Food production in all the developing countries rose by over two and a half per cent annually between 1950 and 1975; but demand for food has grown by well over three per cent a year as populations and incomes have gone up'(91). One result is higher food imports by the South – on current trends, 145 million tonnes by 1990, '80 million of which would be needed by the poorer countries of Africa and Asia'(91). Likely foreign exchange earnings and *Aid* levels will not be enough to pay for 'such massive food imports . . . the suffering, unless something is done, will be appalling'(91).

This is also one of the *Mutual Interests* of North and South, since an inevitable consequence will be higher food prices affecting all countries. A first priority must be all necessary aid for *Agricultural Development* to increase domestic food production in the South. 'Food production grew more slowly than population in 58 out of 106 developing countries during the period 1970–78'(93).

At the same time, there will be a continuing need for imports from the North, where food production policies must take into account the world food situation, not just national interests of producers and consumers.

Foreign Investment

'In 1975 the total stock of direct foreign investment in the developing countries was about $68 billion, about one-fourth of world foreign investment. The annual flows in the mid-1970s were about $8 billion, which is about 12 per cent of the total flow of resources to the Third World. Foreign investment has moved to a limited number of developing countries, mainly those which could offer political stability and a convenient economic environment, including tax incentives, large markets, cheap labour and easy access to oil or other natural resources. Purely financial investments have gone to tax havens in developing countries, which the UN lists as Bahamas, Barbados, Bermuda, Cayman Islands, Netherlands Antilles and Panama. Of the rest, 70 per cent of the investment in the Third World has been in only fifteen countries. Over 20 per cent is in Brazil and Mexico alone and the rest in other middle-income countries in Latin America – Argentina, Peru, Venezuela – or in South-East Asia – Malaysia, Singapore, Hong Kong. About one-quarter is in oil-exporting developing countries. In the poorer countries foreign investment is mainly in plantations and in minerals, or in countries with large internal markets like India. Private investment can supplement and complement *Aid*, but it cannot substitute for it; it tends not to move to the countries or sectors which most need aid'(187).

Free Trade Areas and Common Markets

Free trade areas and common markets are groups of countries which eliminate tariffs (customs duties) on their trade with each other, and usually also pursue other policies of encouraging mutual trade, including action against *Non-Tariff Barriers*. The distinction between the two is that in a free trade area the members each have separate tariffs against non-members, whilst in a common market (or 'community') there is a common external tariff surrounding the group against non-members, and usually a common policy on general matters of economic relations with the rest of the world.

Such associations in the South are all in the Western

hemisphere. They are: the Caribbean Community, of Antigua, Barbados, Belize, Dominica, Grenada, Guyana, Jamaica, Montserrat, St. Kitts-Nevis-Anguilla, Saint Lucia, St. Vincent and Trinidad and Tobago; the Central American Common Market, of El Salvador, Guatemala, Honduras and Nicaragua; and the Latin American Free Trade Association of Argentina, Brazil, Chile, Colombia, Ecuador, Mexico, Paraguay, Peru, Uruguay and Venezuela.

Freight Rates

Ocean freight rates tend to be higher on processed products than on basic commodities. This is one factor hindering the development of processing in the South, which would give the South a bigger share of the total *Added Value* in products (143). *UNCTAD* has given particular attention to the need to increase the South's share in ocean shipping.

GATT – General Agreement on Tariffs and Trade

The General Agreement on Tariffs and Trade established a UN body concerned with rules for fair international trade. It was set up in 1948, with headquarters in Geneva, following the US Congress's failure to ratify the Havana Charter of the International Trade Organization envisaged at Bretton Woods. Its principal activity since then has been the holding of successive rounds of Multilateral Trade Negotiations (MTNs) for tariff-cutting and other trade liberalization measures. The most recent was the Tokyo Round agreed in 1980.

GATT has had a Committee on Trade and Development since 1965 concerned with trade problems of the South. But the creation of *UNCTAD* in 1964 had been 'partly because developing countries felt that GATT did not and could not completely serve them in trying to change the trading system'(184), in view of its emphasis on removing restrictions on trade, when what the South needs is special treatment and preferences.

Generalized System of Preferences

In 1968 a system was negotiated at *GATT* whereby, initially for ten years, countries of the North importing manufactured and processed goods from the South agreed to negotiate special tariff preferences (no tariffs or special low ones) for them. Schemes in operation include that agreed by the *European Community* with members of the Lomé Convention.

Brandt says that improvements should be made in the GSP's operation: rules of origin, exemptions and quota limits should be eased. One step forward is that the Tokyo Round of Multilateral Trade Negotiations under *GATT* has recognized that 'preferential treatment of developing countries should be accepted as a permanent feature of the world trading system rather than as a temporary exception'(183).

Grain Storage
Improvements in grain storage facilities in the South are needed. 'In drought-prone areas in particular where irrigation is not practicable they are essential for ensuring that food is available locally'(96).

Green Revolution
This term is applied to an upsurge in grain production in a number of countries in the 1960s and early 1970s, resulting from new crop varieties and greater use of *Fertilizers*. Brandt comments that it 'has spectacularly increased grain production, but mainly in areas where *Irrigation* was available ... it has been less successful in areas with unpredictable rainfall or in semi-arid regions (including most of sub-Saharan Africa)'(81).

Group of 77
At the first *UNCTAD* Conference in 1964, the Group of 77 developing countries was formed from the *United Nations* groups A and C. Now with over 100 members, the Group is the common bargaining front of the South against the North.

Health
'Human energy and innovation depends on good health'(82). But despite recent improvements most people in the South suffer from poorer health than in the North. *Life Expectancy* is lower, with, particularly, a high infant and child mortality. 'There are still countries in Africa where one child in four does not survive until its first birthday. Blindness afflicts 30 to 40 million people in the Third World and threatens many tens of millions more, whether from river-blindness, vitamin A deficiency or water-borne infections'(55).

Hunger and Malnutrition are prime causes of ill-health, together with the effects of lack of safe *Water Supplies and Sanitation*. Improvement in these background factors such as is aimed for in the *Decade for Drinking Water and Sanitation* is a necessary condition for better health. But improved medical care and control of *Diseases* is needed. The *WHO* Conference on Primary Health Care in 1978 set the target to attain for all people by the year 2000 'a level of health that will permit them to lead a socially and economically productive life'. Brandt comments that 'the costs of raising health services to an acceptable level are in themselves relatively small. The *WHO* estimates that $3 per child would be sufficient to immunize every newborn child in the developing world against the six most common childhood diseases. With present birth rates this amounts to $0.12 per person per year spread over the total population of those countries. To provide primary health care for all might, on the basis of pilot studies, be estimated to cost some $2.50–$4 per person annually'(56).

Housing

The rapid growth of urbanization in the South is the principal cause of a major housing problem, most obvious in the growth of 'shanty towns'. A recent study of a cross section of cities of the South showed that 'one-third to two-thirds of all families could not afford the cheapest new housing currently being built'(56).

Hunger and Malnutrition

'Poverty goes hand in hand with hunger'(90). More than one-fifth of the people of the world are undernourished or hungry, at least 500–600 million, possibly 1 billion. And 'in some low-income countries studies have shown as many as 40 per cent of pre-school children exhibiting clinical signs of malnutrition'(90).

If *Food Production* is to be adequate for needs in the year 2000, 'major efforts of investment, planning and research'(90) will be necessary, with high priority for *Agricultural Development* in the South. 'But not only must the food be there: people who need it must be able to buy it'(91). Brandt insists that 'this Commission sees no more important task before the world community than the elimination of hunger and malnutrition in all countries. Conclusions similar to those we have reached are shared by many other bodies, including most recently the US Presidential Commission on World Hunger. We are well aware that this is not a limited task – it involves nearly all aspects of the world economy and the development process, to create and distribute both the required food and the employment and incomes which will enable the food to be bought by those who need it. But the world has the capacity to achieve such a goal; it is imperative that it does so'(103).

ILO – International Labour Organization

Dating from 1919, it became a UN specialized agency in 1946, with headquarters in Geneva. It is concerned with international employment matters, particularly the establishing of international minimum labour standards and conditions, including the employment of children, women and migrants. It is therefore involved in trade unions' interest in *Fair Labour Standards*. It has a Convention on rural workers' organizations and their role in economic and social development. 1980–81 budget is $203m.

IMF – International Monetary Fund

Set up in 1944 as one of the *Bretton Woods* institutions, the IMF is the nearest equivalent to a world central bank. Its task is to help make monetary relationships between member countries work smoothly. It is not a development institution, but some of its activities are of particular benefit to countries of the South.

The IMF holds funds subscribed as 'quotas' by members, partly in gold and partly in their own currencies. If a member country has a balance of payments deficit, the IMF can make a medium-term loan (usually not more than five years) in a mixture of the currencies it holds and its own currency, the *SDR – Special Drawing Right*. Loans are conditional on the country agreeing with the IMF on economic policies to improve the balance of payments.

Voting rights at the IMF are in proportion to the members' contribution quotas, which are assessed in accordance with each country's general economic weight and role in world trade. The United States has 19.83 per cent of votes, UK 6.93 per cent, Germany (Federal Republic) 5.13 per cent, France 4.57 per cent and so on. So decisions are effectively in the hands of the major industrialized nations of the North.

As well as the general loan facility, the IMF operates certain facilities to deal with particular types of problem, and these tend to be of special interest to the South. *The Compensatory Financing Facility* makes loans to compensate for unexpected falls in export earnings from *Commodities*, and the Buffer Stock Facility finances stocks set up under *International Commodity Agreements*. The extended Loan Facility offers loans for a longer term than usual (up to 10 years) when solving a balance of payments problem requires structural changes in an economy. The Trust Fund is the repository for the profits made by the sale of some of the IMF's gold in the late 1970s, and is to be used to give the poorest nations specially favourable terms in the use of the various facilities.

Brandt wants to see an increase in world liquidity created by the IMF through the issue of SDRs. In the general operations of the IMF, criticisms have been made of the conditions imposed for loans. These tend to emphasize the cutting of domestic demand in debtor countries. 'The Fund's insistence on drastic measures, often within the time framework of only one year, has tended to impose unnecessary and unacceptable political burdens on the poorest, on occasion leading to "IMF riots" and even the downfall of governments'(216). In particular, 'the deficits for which a government can be held responsible should surely be distinguished from those that are due to short-term factors beyond its control' (216). So 'conditions for lending requiring deflationary adjustment – including devaluation policies – should not be imposed by the IMF unless it justifies such action in detail by assessing the probable consequences of deflationary policies for income distribution, employment and social services; and that programmes of adjustment should be more often formulated for periods longer than one year'(217). There should be expansion of the IMF's specific long-term facilities. And the need to stabilize the South's export earnings means that the *Compensatory Financing Facility* should be about three times bigger than at present. If in its operations 'the IMF is trying to take broader development objectives into account, it should also recruit and promote more people from developing countries with appropriate qualifications and sensitivity to the problems involved'(217).

Industrialization
In the South industrialization is generally seen as central to development: 'the drive towards it reflects deeply felt needs for modernization and economic independence'(172). Brandt emphasizes that it must and can go side by side with *Agricultural Development*. 'There need not be a conflict between the priorities of industry and agriculture in a nation's development. They remain closely interdependent, with the income and production from one providing the demand for the other. To manage this critical balance between industry and agriculture and provide healthy conditions in both sectors is one of

the most crucial tasks for the governments of the Third World' (173). Industrial jobs are needed to supplement agricultural under-employment, or for *Landless Labourers* displaced by improvements in agricultural productivity (98).

In the 1970s manufacturing output in the South grew twice as fast as in the North, but the South's share of world manufacturing is still small – around 10 per cent. And it is unevenly distributed. Some middle-income countries in Latin America and South-East Asia 'have about a quarter of their workers in manufactures (as much as some older industrialized countries) ... but in many of the poorest countries the figure is less than five per cent'(172). The 1975 Lima Declaration of the *UN Industrial Development Organization* set the target of a 25 per cent share for the South by the year 2000. This would require an annual growth in manufacturing value added of 10–11 per cent.

Such growth must include more exports from the South, both to the North and within the South itself. Industrialization in the South has tended to begin with highly-protected local industry to substitute for imports. But this, in most countries, provides too small a base for balanced and efficient industrialization. 'Since the 1960s many developing countries have moved towards strategies to promote exports and to offset disadvantages due to the insulation of their domestic markets'(174). So manufactures are now taking a bigger share of exports by countries of the South: 10 per cent of non-fuel exports in 1955, 50 per cent now. *Access to Markets* is therefore vital to continued industrialization.

Inflation
Brandt lays particular stress on the way in which more positive development policies towards the South can help the North to cope with the problem of inflation. Better *Access to Markets* in the North for manufactures from the South can help keep prices low for consumers there. Conversely, protectionism has an inflationary effect. Action to stabilize the prices of *Commodities* can also reduce inflation (71). Brandt believes that the control of inflation is one of the significant respects in which development policies can be in the *Mutual Interests* of North and South.

Informal Sector of the Economy
Urban poverty is particularly found amongst those employed in what has been called the 'informal sector' of the economy, which Brandt defines as 'a myriad of small-scale activities:

repairs, manufacturing, construction, trade, catering and other services'(130). Development policies should pay more attention to the job-growth capability of these activities, through easier credit, training, technical advice, and sub-contracting from larger organizations.

Integrated Programme for Commodities
Adopted at *UNCTAD* IV in Nairobi in 1976, the Programme is intended to comprise the *Common Fund* for financing stocks and the production, processing and marketing of *Commodities* of importance in the South's exports, and more *International Commodity Agreements* on such exports.

Inter-American Development Bank
see *Regional Development Banks*

Intermediate Technology
see *Appropriate Technology*

International Commodity Agreements
The existing International Commodity Agreements (ICAs) between producing and consuming countries cover wheat, sugar, tin, cocoa, coffee and natural rubber. The aim is to stabilize prices through the establishment, where possible, of buffer stocks, and by agreement on export quotas to prevent exporting countries from under-cutting each other on world markets. Under the *Integrated Programme for Commodities* agreed by *UNCTAD*, more ICAs are to be established, and the new *Common Fund* is to improve the financial foundation for the work of existing and new ICAs.

Brandt points out the problems: 'Price ranges have proved difficult to negotiate, adjust and support. Serious considera-tion should be given to such issues as whether minimum prices alone or export taxes might not be more appropriate and easier to negotiate and administer in some circumstances; but action to establish reasonable price floors where possible is highly desirable.' In general, the emphasis for ICAs should 'be on how to make them work more effectively'(130).

International Development Association – IDA
The IDA is an affiliate of the *World Bank*, set up in 1960 to provide loans on 'soft' terms for the poorer developing countries. The eligibility limit is that the country should have a GNP per head of $625 a year or less (in 1978) and most loans

– 87 per cent of total commitments – are to countries below $360 per head. Loans are interest-free, and for 50 years, with a grace period of 10 years before repayments start.

In 1980 the IDA committed $3 838m. in support of 103 projects in 40 countries. Resources come from 121 subscribing members, and are replenished at three-year intervals. Brandt believes that this is too short: 'work on the next replenishment has to begin even before arrangements have been concluded for the previous one. The cycle should be extended, to at least five years'(249).

International Finance Corporation – IFC
The IFC is an affiliate of the *World Bank*, set up in 1956 to provide loans to private enterprises, and to banks and other financial institutions lending to private enterprises, in developing countries. Loans are made in association with private investors. The IFC in 1980 made 55 investments in 30 countries, totalling $681m.

International Fund for Agricultural Development
This fund was set up in 1977 with about $1 billion from industrialized countries and from OPEC, for three years 'to raise food production and consumption by the poorest people in the poorest countries'. Brandt praises its procedures: 'with 124 member countries, its management structure enjoys full participation of developed and developing countries and has taken all its decisions by consensus'(94).

International Grains Arrangement
Negotiations for a new International Grains Arrangement to improve world grain supplies and in particular better *Food Stocks*, with special help for the South, began in 1978 and have stood adjourned through lack of agreement since 1979.

International Monetary System
The instability of the world monetary system since the early 1970s is a problem for both North and South, but increases the special difficulties of the South.

From *Bretton Woods* in 1944, until 1971, nations maintained their currencies at fixed values in exchanges with each other, devaluations and revaluations of parities taking place only rarely. The *IMF – International Monetary Fund* managed the system, providing countries with credits to overcome short-term balance of payments problems. The US dollar played a leading role in the system. In particular, the supply of extra money needed by the world system to finance economic growth – the supply of world liquidity – was mainly provided by dollars exported from the USA and held by other nations. Growing worries about this trend contributed to the breakdown of the system. The dollar was devalued in 1971, and in 1973 the whole system ended.

Since 1973, currencies have fluctuated in value against each other in an international money market. These fluctuations are exaggerated by speculative forces, and are often much greater and more volatile than the underlying real economic changes between countries would justify. The resulting uncertainties affect all countries. Especially, 'developing countries and small industrialized countries find themselves buffeted by the unpredictable ups and downs of the major currencies. They have been faced with major new problems in the management of their own exchange rates, foreign reserves and debt'(205). Reform proposals, notably those of the Committee of Twenty set up in 1972, have produced no real decisions.

Brandt 'believes that the reform of the world monetary system is urgent and must address itself to the following issues: the exchange rate regime, the reserve system (the creation and distribution of the international means of payment or liquidity); and the adjustment mechanism as it affects the countries issuing reserve currencies, surplus countries and deficit countries'(207).

Greater stability of *Exchange Rates* requires first the reforms on the other two issues. But there is also 'need for national policies which both curb inflation and achieve adequate rates of growth and rising employment levels ... exchange rate stability requires both discipline at home and international co-operation to maintain it'(203).

The reserves held by national monetary authorities comprise three elements: gold, other national currencies (especially dollars) and international assets – countries' reserve positions in the IMF plus *SDRs – Special Drawing Rights*. The total of international assets is only one-tenth of the total of reserves held in national currencies. Brandt wants to 'make Special Drawing Rights the principal reserve asset' (273), as was agreed in principle by the Amendment of the IMF Articles agreed at Jamaica in 1976. 'An SDR system would enable a broader and more equitable sharing among countries of the benefits and costs that accompany an international reserve currency. It would also avoid the danger of instability that comes from a multiplicity of reserve currencies'(210).

The world monetary system has to provide an adjustment mechanism to cope with countries' balance of payments surpluses and deficits. This is the basic role of the IMF. 'A reformed system must ensure that both surplus and deficit countries have some obligation to adjust'(213). This must include means 'to encourage countries in current account surpluses to make long-term loans to deficit countries that are undertaking needed adjustment'(214). Above all, the adjustment process should 'not increase contractionist pressures in the world economy. The adjustment process of developing countries should be placed in the context of maintaining long-term economic and social development'(219).

International Trade Organization

Although when the *GATT* Articles were being renewed in 1954–55, the signatories accepted that there was a need for an Organization for Trade Co-operation, to cover a wider range of members and subjects than GATT, nothing came of this. Brandt believes that the need ought to be met, by setting up an International Trade Organization, to encompass the functions of GATT and *UNCTAD*, co-ordinating international agreements in such matters as those relating to *Transnational Corporations*, *Transfer of Technology* and state trading practices (185).

International Taxation

see *Automatic Revenues*

Irrigation

In *Agricultural Development* 'the most fundamental difficulty is control and management of water'. Heavy tropical rains harm crops through flooding, soil leaching, root-zone saturation; in contrast, most African countries 'have much of their farming within semi-arid tropics where evapotranspiration is exceedingly high and rainfall can vary by 40 per cent from year to year'(81).

Predictability of water supply, through irrigation with proper drainage, is 'the most important single measure to encourage farmers to adopt improved farming techniques'. Some major irrigation schemes would be possible in such river basins as Niger, Brahmaputra-Ganges and Mekong, costing at least $50 billion over the next 15–20 years. As well, 'there is also scope for small irrigation projects undertaken by local communities'(81).

Land Reform
see *Agrarian Reform*

Landless Labourers
Although in much of the South the problem of landless agricultural labourers can be tackled by *Agrarian Reform*, in some
countries over-population of cultivable land is too great for that
to be effective. In Bangladesh one-third of the population is
landless, 'yet large holdings account for only 0.2 per cent of the
total land'(86), so the scope for redistribution to the landless is
clearly limited. Higher crops from irrigation and flood control
could increase labour demand, but *Industrialization* to provide
more non-agricultural jobs is also needed.

Least Developed Countries – LLDCs
The concept of 'Least Developed Countries' was recognized at
UNCTAD II (1968) and in the 1971 UN General Assembly.
The 27 LLDCs are defined as countries having particularly
severe long-term constraints on development assessed on three
basic criteria: per capita GDP of $100 or less at 1970 prices, a
share of manufacturing of 10 per cent or less of GDP, and 20 per
cent or less of literate persons aged 15 or more. In 1977 their
total population was 258 million (13 per cent of the total population of developing countries), and their average GDP was $150,
equalling $80 at 1970 prices. GDP per head had grown less than
one per cent a year for the last two decades. Most of these
countries are in what Brandt calls the *Poverty Belts*. The larger
ones, with a population (1978) of 5 million or more, were: Bangladesh – 83.64m.; Ethiopia – 31.01m.; Sudan – 17.39m.; Tanzania – 16.87m; Afghanistan – 14.62m.; Nepal – 13.63m.;
Uganda – 12.42m.; Mali – 6.30m.; Malawi – 5.78m.; Guinea –
5.13m.; Niger – 5.01m.

Levy on International Trade
see *Automatic Revenues*

Life Expectancy
Average life expectancy in the North is more than 70 years; in
the South it is nearer 50 for most people. But there have been
significant improvements over the last two decades, mainly as a
result of disease control. 'In large parts of South and East Asia,
in North Africa and the Middle East, people can expect to live
10 to 15 years longer'(54). This, however, has added to the
problem of *Population Growth*.

Literacy

One-third of the adults in the South were literate in 1950: now it is a little over half. The rise was from 65 per cent in 1960 to 75 per cent in 1970 in Latin America, from 45 to 53 per cent in Aia, and from 20 to 26 per cent in Africa. There are still 34 countries where illiteracy is over 80 per cent: and in the following 14 countries it is 90 per cent or more – Afghanistan, Chad, Guinea, Ethiopia, Gambia, Guinea-Bissau, Mali, Mauritania, Niger, Oman, Senegal, Sierra Leone, Togo and Upper Volta.

Lomé Agreement

The arrangements for trade preferences and other forms of development assistance between the *European Community* and 60 African, Caribbean and Pacific (ACP) countries were settled in the 'Lomé II' Agreement, running from 1980 to 1985 – the second such agreement.

Manpower Training

Provision for manpower training enters into the development process in two ways. For the South itself, it is important as part of *Industrialization*, and of the increase in *Absorptive Capacity* for development funds, by providing more persons able to carry out the necessary projects and activities. For the North, it is necessary as part of the *Restructuring of Industry* that must take place to accommodate more imports from the South.

Massive Transfers

see *Development Finance*

Migrant Workers

About 20 million workers in the world have migrated across national frontiers; 12 million of these workers are from developing countries. Principal receiving areas are the United States (6 million), Western Europe (5 million), and more recently the Middle East oil exporters (3 million). Most migrant workers are unskilled or semi-skilled, often recruited for jobs that local workers find distasteful or underpaid. But there is also a 'brain drain' of over 400 000 Third World people with professional qualifications working in richer countries.

Sending countries benefit from remittances ($7 billion a year from Western Europe and $5 billion from the Middle East), often a major source of foreign exchange, and from the industrial skills workers may come home with. Receiving countries benefit from a labour force that is treated as disposable when economies fluctuate, and has fewer rights generally than local workers. This is accentuated by the fact that many migrants are employed illegally without proper occupational and social welfare.

The *International Labour Organisation* (ILO) has set up rules about fair treatment for migrant workers and their families, in social security, health, safety, unity of families, preservation of ethnic identity and trade union rights. Very few countries have yet signed. Brandt recommends more international agreement on control of migration and ensuring mutual benefits to all countries involved, along lines indicated at the World Employment Conference in 1976 (111).

The IMF *Compensatory Financing Facility* includes help to countries in coping with fluctuations in migrants' remittances received.

Minerals

One of the most important matters in which North and South have *Mutual Interests* is in ensuring adequate future supplies of minerals. Setting aside the particular problem of *Oil Production,* Brandt believes there should be no general scarcity of minerals in the rest of this century, though noting that the Leontieff Report to the UN in 1977 'suggested that lead and zinc, and possibly also nickel and copper, might become scarce by the end of the century'. But beyond that date, general problems may develop. Current minerals exploration is inadequate for future needs – 'in the last few years as much as 80 to 90 per cent of the spending in exploration has been concentrated in a very few of the developed or *Newly Industrializing Countries,* whereas it has almost entirely ceased over large areas of the Third World'(155).

Brandt finds the reason for this in a breakdown of confidence between countries of the South and the *Transnational Corporations* who control most mineral exploration and production. Minerals exploration always has to be undertaken as a venture with no guarantee of commercial success. Countries of the South 'are now reluctant to sign these resources away in far-reaching concession agreements negotiated at a time when they know little of the extent and richness of their own potential discoveries, and when their negotiating position *vis-à-vis* an exploration company is certain to be weak. Mining companies, however, are unwilling to sink money in major exploration ventures in developing countries unless the full terms on which any discovery is to be exploited are fully negotiated in advance and, preferably, guaranteed by an international body'(155).

To end this impasse, Brandt concludes that more finance should be made available through a multilateral financing facility for exploration in the South, so that mining agreements need be made only when everybody concerned knows the value of the deposits, and the finance could then be 'converted into a loan and part of the initial financing of the project if a commercial deposit is discovered, developed and exploited'(157). Although the *UN Revolving Fund for Natural Resource Exploitation* 'goes some way towards meeting this requirement', Brandt believes that its repayment terms are too onerous for poor countries.

The institution running such a financing facility could also provide the South with technical assistance in such matters as mining law and in negotiations over concessions.

Multi-Fibre Arrangement – MFA

The MFA is a set of quotas and other trade restrictions limiting the growth of imports of *Textiles* into the *European Community* from countries of the South other than most of those associated with the Community under the *Lomé Agreement*, and also from certain Mediterranean and East European countries. It is made under the provisions of *GATT* for *Safeguards on Imports*. The current Arrangement expires at the end of 1981, and is certain to be extended in at least as restrictive a form.

From 1976 to 1979 imports of MFA products from the countries covered rose by an average of 4 per cent a year in volume, compared with 25 per cent a year from 1973 to 1976. But it is pointed out in the South that imports from those countries of the South that are restricted by the MFA have grown more slowly than those from European countries outside the Community, whilst the imports from the USA, not covered by the MFA, which is the largest single exporter of MFA products to the Community, rose by 65 per cent from 1978 to 1979. Brandt comments that 'the Multi-Fibre arrangement . . . which stipulates that import quotas should grow by at least 6 per cent per year, has been rendered less effective by unilateral restrictions'(177).

Multilateral Trade Negotiations
see *GATT*

Mutual Interests

Brandt particularly emphasizes that the development of the South is in the mutual interests of North and South alike. 'This principle of mutuality of interest has been at the centre of our discussions.' Human solidarity and a commitment to international social justice are basic motives, especially for the aid consisting of 'grant-like flows to the poorest countries and regions'(75). But they can be buttressed by motives of enlightened self-interest for the North. These are partly economic, partly concerned with world stability and peace.

The economic argument starts from the fact that development of the South can be an 'engine of growth' for the whole world economy. But why should governments of the North, 'hesitant to stimulate their own economies in a period of stagflation, find more virtue in a process of stimulation which operates via the developing countries?'(67).

One suggested answer is that such stimulus which increases international trade thereby increases the efficiency with which economies operate, through greater specialization and higher productivity. It is therefore a less inflationary form of economic expansion than is purely domestic stimulation in a particular country.

This is linked with the argument that it is against the interests of Northern countries for them to try to cope with economic difficulty by trade protection, especially against cheap manufactures from the South, because *Protectionism* adds to inflation. And, more importantly, North–South trade is a two-way process, in which the North enjoys a positive balance of trade in manufactures with the South, so more Northern jobs stand to be lost than to be gained through protection. Better *Access to Markets* in the North by the South will increase imports from the North and generate jobs there.

Similarly, though improvements in *Commodities* marketing and prices are primarily intended to give the South a higher and more stable income, the North will benefit from greater predictability of prices. Brandt notes that commodity price cycles tend to be inflationary through the ratchet effect where other prices go up as commodities do, but are sticky when commodities fall. And the North has a long-term interest in stimulating future supplies of minerals and other raw materials by better prices for the South now.

These arguments apply mainly to relations with the better-off countries of the South, especially the *Newly Industrializing*

Countries. But general arguments of mutual interest apply to all North–South relations.

An even more important matter than economic arguments is that of the world physical *Environment*. Action taken by poor countries may affect all of us – the climatic consequences of *Deforestation* are a major example. Most fundamental of all is the general interest in the preservation of peace, in the face of the likely destabilizing effects of, say, the pressures resulting from *Population Growth*. 'We cannot believe the world can live in peace ... if large sections of the South ... are shut out from any real prospect of progress'(75).

New International Economic Order

The concept originated as a term in the *Algiers Action Programme*, and represented the aim of a fundamental restructuring of the world economy to benefit the South. The basic Declaration was agreed by the UN General Assembly in May 1974. It contained 20 principles dealing with the recognition of the fact of economic interdependence in the world, especially in the relationships between developed and developing countries, and the putting of these and all other international economic relationships onto a basis of equality and co-operation. A Programme of Action was adopted, dealing with: raw materials, *Commodities* and trade; the *World Monetary System* and *Development Finance*; *Industrialization*; *Transfer of Technology*; *Transnational Corporations*; economic rights and duties of states; *Economic Co-operation Between Developing Countries*; sovereignty over natural resources; strengthening the role of the United Nations system; and special measures to help developing countries in the then current economic crisis. A consequential *Charter of Economic Rights and Duties of States* was adopted in December 1974.

Newly Industrializing Countries – NICs

Some countries of the South have enjoyed rapid growth of manufacturing output, to the point where they are now significant in world exports of manufactures. They have achieved high sustained economic growth rates, typically in the 5 to 9 per cent range. These Newly Industrializing Countries (NICs) are principally in South-East Asia and Latin America. Their future prospects depend on their *Access to Markets* in the North and on the policies of the *Transnational Corporations* whose pursuit of international division of labour has been important in the growth of the NICs.

The *Development Assistance Committee* identifies 7 countries of the South as NICs. With their 1978 GNP per capita, they are: Singapore – $3260; Hong Kong – $3040; Argentina – $1910; Brazil – $1570; Taiwan – $1400; Mexico – $1290; Korea, Rep. – $1160. (The DAC list also includes four European countries defined as 'Developing', but not in the Brandt 'South': Spain – $3520; Greece – $3270; Yugoslavia – $2390; Portugal – $2020.)

Non-Tariff Barriers
Tariffs against imports of manufactures have fallen sharply in most countries over the last two decades, as a result of international negotiations through *GATT*. And the countries of the South in some cases benefit from extra reductions under the *Generalized System of Preferences*. But it has become recognised at GATT that non-tariff barriers remain a major obstacle to trade, often more so now than tariffs. They can include 'formal or informal quotas, government subsidies or purchases restricted to their own domestic companies' (42), excessively rigorous application of technical standards requirements, or simply unduly slow administration of import procedures. Certain aspects of trade structures can also serve as non-tariff barriers, such as the effect that *Freight Rates* are said to have on the ocean-borne trade of the South with the North.

Nuclear Energy
see *Alternative Energy Sources*

Ocean Exploitation
In recent decades there has been growing interest in the recovery of ocean-bed minerals, especially the manganese nodules found in the deep ocean area outside nation states' 'exclusive economic zones'. Brandt recommends that revenues from such exploitation (perhaps $500 million a year in the middle or late 1980s) should be reserved for *Automatic Revenues* of development aid.

OECD – Organization for Economic Co-operation and Development
OECD changed to this name in 1960, from the Organization for European Economic Co-operation (EEC), the body set up in 1974 to run the Marshall Plan. It is the principal economic organization of the industrialized countries of the North. Members are: Australia, Austria, Belgium, Canada, Denmark, Finland, France, the Federal Republic of Germany, Greece,

Iceland, Ireland, Italy, Japan, Luxembourg, the Netherlands, New Zealand, Norway, Portugal, Spain, Sweden, Switzerland, Turkey, the United Kingdom and the United States.

Its establishing Convention emphasizes the OECD's world role. It shall promote policies designed:

– to achieve the highest sustainable economic growth and employment and a rising standard of living in member countries, while maintaining financial stability, and thus to contribute to the development of the world economy;
– to contribute to sound economic expansion in member as well as non-member countries in the process of economic development;
– to contribute to the expansion of world trade on a multilateral, non-discriminatory basis in accordance with international obligations.

The *Development Assistance Committee* of OECD comprises those members who have agreed 'to secure an expansion of aggregate volume of resources made available to developing countries and to improve their effectiveness'. The DAC does not act as a development agency itself: its purpose is to improve, harmonize and co-ordinate aid policies and programmes of its members. Of the members of OECD, Greece, Iceland, Ireland, Luxembourg, Portugal, Spain and Turkey are *not* members of the DAC: the Commission of the European Economic Community is a member, and there are observers from the IMF and World Bank.

Official Aid
see *Aid*

Oil and Gas Production
Although in the long term *Alternative Energy Sources* must replace oil, 'about one-quarter of the world's commercial energy today is oil produced by *OPEC* countries ... in the short run any expansion in world energy has to be met chiefly by oil'(163), with the Middle East as the main source. For most of the producer countries in that area there are strong economic and technical arguments for limiting production rates and spreading the depletion of reserves over as long a period as possible.

So more exploration should be undertaken in the South outside the Middle East. At present, 'drilling density in prospective oil areas in industrialized countries is about forty times that in those of the oil-importing developing countries'. But as with *Minerals* generally, 'the mutual distrust between the major oil companies and many developing countries is a serious obstacle'. Arrangements for 'fair negotiation and security' are urgently necessary(164).

Oil Prices

The price increases brought about by *OPEC* quadrupled the price of oil in 1973–74. The result was a sudden deterioration in the balances of payments of the oil-importing countries, with an impact that was particularly severe on the poorer countries of the South who are in any case liable to suffer persistent balance of payments deficits because of their growth efforts. Some of the resulting surpluses in the hands of OPEC countries have been used for aid through the *Arab Aid Agencies* and direct, but most have been *Recycled* through the international banking system and mainly lent back to countries of the South. This does not, however, eliminate the impact, since it creates a heavy *Debt Repayment Burden*.

The problem was then compounded by further increases in oil prices in 1979 (46 per cent) and 1980 (60 per cent). This meant that the oil import bill of the *Least Developed Countries* rose from $690m. in 1978 to $1520m. in 1980 (OECD estimates), and the total for all oil-importing developing countries rose from $31700m. to $67500m. Largely in consequence of these increases throughout the 1970s, the current balance of payments deficits of these countries as a group rose from 1.8 per cent of GNP in 1973 to 4.5 per cent in 1980.

Brandt's recommendations on *Energy* are dominated by the need to tackle the oil problem. 'There must be an accommodation between oil-producing and consuming countries which can ensure more secure supplies, more rigorous conservation, more predictable changes of prices and more positive measures to develop alternative sources of energy'(278).

OPEC – Organization of Petroleum Exporting Countries

OPEC was set up in 1960 'to unify and co-ordinate members' petroleum policies and to safeguard their interests generally', and in particular to maintain *Oil Prices* 'with due regard to the interests of securing a steady income to the producing countries, an efficient, economic and regular supply of this source of energy to consuming nations and a fair return on capital to those investing in the petroleum industry'. During the 1960s OPEC had little effect on the low-price policies pursued by the oil companies. But in 1973–74 it was able to quadruple oil prices, and double them again in 1978–79.

In consequence, some OPEC countries with small populations have very high per capita incomes. But Brandt points out that this is not true of all of them: 'Indonesia and Nigeria are far from wealthy – between them they have over 200 million people, and huge development problems for which oil revenues provide only a partial solution', whilst almost all the oil exporters have a 'need to create a balanced productive economy to sustain their populations in the future when there will be little oil left'(54).

The members of OPEC at the end of 1980, in descending order of their 1978 per capita GNP, were: Kuwait – $14 890; Saudi Arabia – $8 040; Libya – $6 910; United Arab Emirates – $4 230; Gabon – $3 580; Venezuela – $2 910; Qatar – $2 740; Iran – $2 030; Iraq – $1 860; Algeria – $1 260; Ecuador – $910; Nigeria – $560; Indonesia – $360.

Commenting on the *Recycling of Funds* from OPEC countries, and the aid that has gone from them through the *Arab Aid Agencies* and direct, Brandt points out that 'it is very encouraging that the OPEC countries have, with their increased revenue in recent years, contributed nearly 3 per cent of their GNP' in aid. 'Their effort is specially noteworthy because, in their case, aid does not result in export orders to the donor'(224). But there should be more flows direct or through aid and development agencies: 'rising OPEC revenues should provide enlarged scope for triangular arrangements in setting up projects in developing countries with finance from capital-surplus countries and technology from industrialized or other developing countries'(137).

OPEC countries are also trying to improve their ability to guarantee supplies of oil to poorer countries in the South – see *Energy*.

Patents

Attempts are being made by the *Group of 77* to persuade the industrialized countries to agree to a revision of the 1883 Paris Agreement for the Protection of Industrial Property, which governs the international enforcement of patent rights. The complaint is that companies from the North take out patents for their products in the South but do not produce there or allow their patented products to be produced by local firms. This hinders the *Transfer of Technology* and the growth of

Industrialization in the South. What is being demanded is that developing countries should be free to give the right to use patented technology to others if the owner does not operate it for three years, and to revoke patents not used for two years thereafter.

Pearson Commission
Following a World Bank initiative, a Commission was set up in 1968, chaired by Lester B. Pearson, former Canadian Prime Minister, to review progress in development assistance and propose improved policies. In its 1969 report, says Brandt, 'aid questions occupied much of its attention, which reflected the prevailing philosophy in development circles'(39), but they also stressed *Mutual Interests* in lending.

Planning
To ensure effective policy formulation and implementation, Brandt says 'the importance of efficient planning and economic management can hardly be overemphasized'(132). This involves training of people in planning, management and other organizational skills. This will, however, 'need to be accompanied by efforts to encourage people to organize themselves. There must be emphasis on decentralizing development activities. No system lacking in genuine and full participation of the people will be fully satisfactory or truly effective'(133). India's Five-Year Plans are an example of systematic planning for development.

Pollution
see *Ecology* and *Environment*

Population Growth
Although world fertility has recently declined, so that population growth rates have fallen, by the year 2000 world population will be between 6 and 6.5 billion, from 4.3 billion now. Ninety per cent of the increase will be in the Third World, particularly in its cities – some will be over 30 million by then. Continued decline in world fertility now cannot greatly affect the next two decades, but is relevant to whether and at what level world population will stabilize in the next century – somewhere between 8 and 15 billion is likely, with most Third World populations at least doubling. Such growth is a major burden on development. And 'it is difficult to avoid the conclusion that a world of 15 billion people would be racked by a

host of potentially devastating economic, social and political conflicts'(106).

More than 60 countries with 95 per cent of Third World population have family planning programmes. Successes include China, which in one decade has reduced its growth rate from 2.3 per cent to just over one per cent, and aims at zero growth in the year 2000. A World Fertility Survey of fourteen developing countries found falls in most. Between 75 and 90 per cent of women knew of family planning methods.

Brandt argues that although 'expanded and more efficient family planning services are needed'(107) with international support (at present the *United Nations Fund for Population Activities* can meet only two-thirds of requests), such services, in order to be effective, must be accompanied by general economic and social progress. 'In the final analysis it is development itself that will provide the most propitious environment for stabilizing the world's population at tolerable levels'(108). And Brandt adds that this has been particularly so in countries where the benefits of development are spread widely through the population: the impact of development on birth rates is less where the benefits go mainly to a few.

Poverty

'Many hundreds of millions of people in the poorer countries are pre-occupied solely with survival and elementary needs'(49). The World Bank estimates that 800 million people are living in destitution, so 'almost 40 per cent of the people in the South are surviving . . . with incomes judged insufficient to secure the basic necessities of life'(50).

This destitution is still mainly a rural phenomenon. Mass urban poverty is growing, but is generally 'one step up from rural deprivation'(50). Most of the 800 million live in the *Least Developed Countries*, including Bangladesh, or in the three other large low-income Asian countries, India, Pakistan and Indonesia: many live in the *Poverty Belt* countries. For them there is little scope for relieving poverty by income redistribution. 100 million live in Latin America, and it is here particularly, Brandt says, that some of the richer countries could do more to relieve extreme poverty.

'Recent World Bank projections . . . suggest that there will still be 600 million absolute poor in the countries of the South by the year 2000.'(51)

Poverty Belts

Brandt identifies two 'poverty belts' which contain most of the *Least Developed Countries*. 'One extends across the middle of Africa, from the Sahara in the north to Lake Nyasa in the south. The other, beginning with the two Yemens and Afghanistan, stretches eastwards across South Asia and some East Asian countries' (78). Brandt makes the point that parts of some other countries should be considered as being in the poverty belts, and receive the same special attention as the *Least Developed Countries*.

Preferential Trading Schemes

The establishment of preferential trading schemes amongst groups of countries of the South is one of the means of promoting *Economic Co-operation Amongst Developing Countries*.

Price Stabilization

see *Commodities* and *Stabex*

Project Lending v. Programme Lending

Most *Aid* is provided for specific projects. Brandt advocates more 'programme lending – providing flexibly usable funds which are not tied to specific investment projects'. Project lending tends to be inflexible, encouraging large capital-intensive projects, with relatively little local content. Programme lending enables a country to use and develop its own resources more. Also, the improvement of social and administrative infrastructures, necessary as a framework for effective development, is not usually covered by project lending.

Brandt argues for a less rigid distinction between temporary assistance, from the *IMF*, and longer-term borrowing: a 'bridge' is needed 'in the form of long-term programme lending'. A context is required of 'well-conceived, clearly defined development programmes, the fulfilment of which can be monitored', to overcome the fear by lending countries that aid not tied to specific projects is more likely to be misused (232–234). The Brandt recommendation that the IMF and World Bank should give more emphasis to 'structural adjustment' in countries of the South is concerned with the need for programme lending.

Protectionism
see *Access to Markets, Non-Tariff Barriers* and *Safeguards on Imports*

Recycling of Funds
In the period after 1974, when most oil-exporting countries developed large balance of payments surpluses, most of the money was invested in the North, mainly through the international commercial banks. The greater part was in turn lent by those banks to the better-off countries in the South. Brandt points out (67) that this 'recycling' (i.e. re-lending) of the surpluses meant that they were mostly transformed into export orders for manufactures from the North. This very much reduced the deflationary impact of the oil price increase on the economies of the North.

Brandt quotes (238) an EEC Commission report stating that had developing countries not borrowed this money and kept their economies expanding, but instead had cut their imports of manufactured goods to meet the increased oil prices, there would have been three million more unemployed in the OECD countries. The consequence of this policy of helping to support the world economy has been, however, that the non-oil producing countries of the South now mostly have a heavy *Debt Repayment Burden*.

Refugees and Displaced Persons
There are about 10 million people who are 'political or religious refugees or who have been displaced by wars and political upheavals'(112), with a world average recently of 2000–3000 new ones a day.

The Universal Declaration of Human Rights states everyone's right to leave their country and seek asylum from persecution elsewhere. The UN Commissioner for Refugees works with voluntary organizations to try to implement this right, to provide temporary care for refugees, and aims at acceptable permanent arrangements. These tasks are made increasingly difficult by the effects of *Population Growth*, whether in rural pressure on scarce land or urban pressure on scarce jobs. Brandt expects the problem to grow 'until the principle of international burden sharing is accepted globally'(113).

Regional Co-operation and Integration

Brandt notes a 'stronger emphasis on mutual co-operation' amongst the countries of the South, in their efforts towards greater self-reliance instead of economic dependence on the North. This shows up in trade. 'The trade of developing countries with one another is growing faster than their trade with the North. In 1976, 22 per cent of the South's total exports and 32 per cent of its exports of manufactured goods went to the South'(88). This trend should be encouraged, not least because it avoids the problem of protectionism in the North. And 'some developing countries have become competitive producers of particular capital goods. India exports heavy machinery, electric pylons and whole factories'(137).

Such trade is, however, hampered by the fact that historical links mean that physical and financial facilities for trade tend to favour North–South patterns. Encouragement is needed for regional and sub-regional *Preferential Trading Arrangements* to alter these old patterns. And these 'need to be complemented by better pooling of regional resources to establish joint industries'(136) for countries with small domestic markets. The problem is partly one of planning and executing aid and development on a regional scale. Brandt commends the role of the regional economic commissions such as the *Economic Commission for Africa* and the *Economic and Social Commission for Asia and the Pacific*, as well as informal groupings such as the Club du Sahel, a 'very flexible association between member countries and donor agencies'(87). Regional monetary arrangements should be encouraged. Trade within the South would be helped if better *Export Finance* were available.

Another recommendation is that 'the *Regional Development Banks* should play a more important role in development lending'(250) – at present they provide about one-fourth of multilateral lending to their regions. They need more capital, and should undertake more *Programme Lending* as well as their more customary *Project Lending*.

Regional Development Banks

These banks are smaller versions of the *World Bank*: their capital is subscribed by member countries in the same way and they lend for the same purposes and on the same lines. But they are independent of the World Bank, though sometimes they work with it on particular projects. 'At present the regional banks provide about one-fourth of multilateral lending to their regions, while the balance comes mainly from the World Bank'(250).

They are:

1) Inter-American Development Bank, set up in 1959, headquarters in Washington. Members are principally from the Organization of American States, but also include Canada, and certain European 'non-regional' members. There are 41 in all. The authorized capital is $11 200m.
2) African Development Bank, set up in 1963, headquarters in Abidjan (Ivory Coast). There are 49 members. Authorized capital is $1 300m. The African Development Fund is a concessional ('soft') loans subsidiary, with 22 members, and resources of about $1 200m.
3) Asian Development Bank, set up in 1966, headquarters in Manila (Philippines). There are 29 regional members and 14 non-regional (of whom 7 are members of the European Community). Authorized capital is $9 400m. The Asian Development Fund is a concessional loans subsidiary, with resources exceeding $2 000m. There is also a Technical Assistance General Fund.
4) Arab Fund for Economic and Social Development, one of the *Arab Aid Agencies*. Its commitments made in 1978 totalled $895m.

Linked to the regional banks are a number of sub-regional ones, mostly associated with *Free Trade Areas and Common Markets* and similar regional groupings. These are the Central American Bank for Economic Integration, the Caribbean Development Bank, the East African Bank and the West African Development Bank.

Brandt says that these regional and sub-regional banks 'should play a more important role in development lending. They should be ready to lend for Programmes no less than projects' (see *Project Lending* v. *Programme Lending*) 'and give more importance to strengthening domestic and regional capabilities . . . they are in a position to have a closer awareness of the needs of their borrowing members' than the World Bank, but 'they lack the funds and the long expertise of the World Bank, if they are to become broader sources of finance. Provided that they are appropriately reformed, the objective should be to achieve a more equal position for regional banks *vis-à-vis* the World Bank in the next decade'(249).

Restructuring of Industry

The demands of industrial change require a continuous process of restructuring of industrial economies as old industries contract and new ones develop. In the North, part of the stimulus to industrial change is the need to accomodate the shift whereby some activities can more appropriately be carried out in the South. 'Restructuring is always needed as nations change their relative competitiveness, but it is also required for domestic economic efficiency'(35). Brandt emphasizes that it is part of the *Mutual Interests* of North and South that the North should try to meet this challenge, not negatively by protectionism, but positively by active measures such as *Manpower Training* to ease restructuring of industry and guide it into areas of expansion. Where countries introduce *Safeguards on Imports* these should be subject to international agreement conditional on positive plans for industrial restructuring, with 'specific time schedules, for example over a five-year period, for phasing out uncompetitive parts of industry'(182). The context of such measures must be a restructuring of the world economy and its balance between North and South.

Safeguards on Imports

Article 19 of *GATT* allows countries to impose trade restrictions if an increase in imports has caused or threatens 'serious injury' to domestic producers. Exporting countries must be notified and consulted, and restrictions maintained only 'to the extent and for such time as may be necessary to prevent or remedy such injury'. In practice, barriers by the North against imports from the South have violated Article 19, often in the guise of 'voluntary export restraints' or 'orderly marketing arrangements' which have taken advantage of the North's bargaining power.

Brandt wants the limitations to be strengthened, with a necessity for multilateral agreement. 'Safeguard measures must be explicit, of limited duration and gradually phased out'(180). The emphasis must be on linkage of safeguards with *Restructuring of Industry* in the importing country on a definite time schedule.

Sanitation

see *Water Supplies and Sanitation*

SDRs – Special Drawing Rights

SDRs are the IMF's own currency-equivalent, issued to IMF members from time to time in proportion to their fund quotas, and comprising part of any loan made by the Fund. They can be exchanged through the IMF for national currencies, or held by a country as a reserve asset. They are only traded between central banks (and the Bank of International Settlements); they are not used in commercial transactions.

The 1976 Jamaica Agreement on amendment to the IMF articles included the aim of 'making the Special Drawing Right the principal reserve asset in the international monetary system', in the place of national currencies used for reserve purposes by other countries, and in place of gold. But, says Brandt, 'the SDR can only be the centrepiece of the international monetary system if it becomes the principal means of increasing global liquidity and if it is itself used to improve the adjustment mechanism'(210).

The argument for increasing the use of SDRs in the *International Monetary System* is a general one, aimed at the benefit of all countries, and is not in itself a North-South matter. But Brandt argues that in the process of achieving the aim of increasing world liquidity as necessary, by the issue of SDRs, there should be an 'SDR link'. This arises from the argument that 'new reserves should be allocated to those countries which are most likely to experience balance of payments deficits and high domestic costs of adjustments ... Many developing countries fit into these categories ... There is therefore a strong case based on efficiency as well as equity for a larger share of new unconditional reserves to be distributed to the developing countries than is achieved through allocations proportional to the IMF quota system'(212).

Brandt stresses that there is no intention of allowing this to have an inflationary effect. 'Our concept of a link would not involve creating any more SDRs than would be warranted by the total reserve needs of the world economy, nor does it mix aid with monetary issues. Given the prevailing rate of interest which is paid by users of SDRs, the concessional element of an SDR allocation is low ... but distributing SDRs more equitably, in a way that is not circumscribed by existing quotas, would provide the developing countries with more of the liquidity which they need and which others can acquire from other sources'(212).

Sea-bed Authority
The 1979 agreement in principle at the *Law of the Sea Conference* that an international sea-bed authority should be set up to deal with matters of *Ocean Exploitation* has not yet been put into effect.

Soil Erosion
see *Deforestation*

Solar Energy
see *Alternative Energy Sources*

Stabex
Under the *Lomé Convention* between the European Community and 60 African, Caribbean and Pacific countries, Stabex is an export earnings stabilization scheme. It covers 29 commodities. If a country's receipts from exporting a particular commodity to the EEC drop below the preceding four-year average, the difference is made up by a low-interest loan, to be paid back when earnings rise again. For the 34 poorest countries, the payment is an outright grant. *Stabex* does not include *Minerals*: these are covered by a new $380 million minerals assistance scheme of very soft loans – 40 years at one per cent – to maintain production and exports of six minerals where ACP countries are dependent on them.

Technical Co-operation Between Developing Countries
The countries of the South can improve their industries by sharing technological capabilities, especially where skills and methods are more relevant for other countries of the South than technology from the North. 'In such initiatives the more industrially advanced developing countries like India, Brazil and Yugoslavia can take a lead'(138). Because use of particular technology often results from consultancy advice, Brandt urges wider use of consultancy services from the South. The *UN Development Programme* gives special attention to encouraging technical co-operation.

Terms of Trade
In the 1950s there was concern in the South at what appeared to be a tendency for the prices of *Commodities* to fall, or rise more slowly, compared to the prices of the manufactures that

commodity producers had to import from the North. It appears that the mid-1950s to early 1970s were such a period, but it is now more likely that the future terms of trade will move in favour of commodities, taking one year with another. Brandt believes that the main concern should not be with long-term trends but with short- and medium-term periods when the 'vagaries of the market' produce low prices which harm producing countries, and, by discouraging investment needed now to meet future requirements, also harm the consuming countries in the long run (147).

Textiles and Clothing

Textiles and clothing are the manufactures which the South has exported most successfully to the North. Brandt points out: 'In the mid-1970s [the South's] share of apparent consumption in the EEC, United States, Canada and Japan reached 7.2 per cent ... Yet even in this area the impact on unemployment in industrialized countries is much less than that of domestic technological change'(176). Despite this, protectionist pressures in the European Community led to the *Multi-Fibre Arrangement* limiting the growth of textile imports into the EEC from the South.

Third World

This term for the developing countries, for which Brandt has substituted 'The South', has no agreed derivation. It is sometimes taken to mean the 'non-aligned' countries, separate from the West and the East. Another explanation is that the term originated as the French *Tiers Monde* because of a suggested parallel between the poor countries of the world and the *Tiers Etat* – the Third Estate, or Commons, in the French Revolution. A drawback of the term is that it may leave the thought in people's minds that the 'Third World' is a third *of* the world, when in fact it accounts for three-quarters of the world's population.

Trade Unions

Trade unions in the North wish to see *Fair Labour Standards* in the South, to ensure that competition against their members' jobs is not based on exploitive wages and conditions. They are keen to ensure that trade unions are allowed and encouraged to develop in the industries of the South. Brandt says 'the international trade union movement is also concerned to ensure that the flows and functioning of private capital are beneficial; increased co-operation among trade unions in different countries can create a better equilibrium in the relations between transnational corporations and governments' (190).

Transfer of Technology

'The sharing of technology is a world-wide concern ... But clearly it is most important to the developing countries; and it can even be argued that their principal weakness is the lack of access to technology, or of command of it' (193). Some information about technology is publicly available, and Brandt recommends that international organizations should do more to enable potential users of information to know where to go for what. But most of the technology the South needs is transmitted commercially, particularly by the *Transnational Corporations*. And, as Brandt explains, 'the market for technology is very imperfect. To the seller, the marginal cost in the sale of an already developed technology may be small although the use may be very profitable to him: the cost to the buyer of doing without it, or developing it on its own, could be very high. The range between the two is so high that it is relative bargaining strength which essentially determines the price; and in this market the developing countries find themselves in an inherently weak negotiating position because of their overwhelming dependence on technology from the North [which] accounts for about 96 per cent of the world's spending on research and development' (194).

Brandt recommends various approaches to improving the South's bargaining power. First, *Aid* should be given without strings tying it to particular sources and, therefore, often to particular technologies. There should be more emphasis on helping *Technical Co-operation Between Developing Countries*. The work of *UNCTAD* in attempting to limit the restrictive effect of patents on use of technology by the South is important. And in all this, there should be emphasis on ensuring the use of *Appropriate Technology* suited to the South's particular needs. The existing efforts 'to formulate codes on the transfer of technology in *UNCTAD*, in the *UN Centre for Transnational Corporations* and in discussions in several other international forums' (195) should be vigorously pursued.

Transfer Prices
see *Transfer Corporations*

Transnational Corporations

'The transnational corporations, or, as they are also called, multinational corporations, are closely involved in many of the areas which are dealt with in this Report: with *Minerals, Commodities, Industrialization, Food* and *Energy* ... They control between a quarter and a third of all world production and are particularly active in processing and marketing. The total sales of their foreign affiliates in 1976 were estimated at $830 billion, which is about the same as the then total GNP of all developing countries excluding oil-exporters'(187). They are important in *Foreign Investment* in the South, though often they provide technology, management or marketing expertise and borrow money locally.

Problems about the role of transnational corporations include the matter of 'transfer pricing'. The 'intra-firm trade' carried on within the transnationals between parent firms and affiliates 'is thought to make up over 30 per cent of all world trade'(188). The prices at which such trade takes place can be fixed by the transnationals so as 'to shift profits from high to low tax countries or to get around exchange or price controls or customs duties'(189). The transnationals can also impose restrictive trade practices, such as allocation of markets, that hamper development in host countries. And there have been allegations that unethical political and commercial activities of some transnationals have encouraged *Corruption* in the South. Concern about these and other problems led to the establishment of the *UN Centre on Transnational Corporations*.

Brandt identifies the central problem as being that 'the developing countries, particularly the smaller and poorer ones, need to improve their bargaining strength. This would lead to a more stable relationship with corporations as it would help to dispel distrust and increase confidence'. It would be in the *Mutual Interests* of all. 'When transnational corporations have at the outset made inequitable contracts with developing countries – particularly in *Minerals* – the result has often been that the contracts have run into trouble. We believe strongly that there is a close connection between the equity and stability of investments'(193).

International agencies should, by information and assistance, help countries of the South to improve their bargaining position. In particular the South should be helped to 'unpackage the "technology-investment package", separating out the components of investment, technology, management and marketing, importing only what they need and using their domestic inputs wherever they can'(191).

There is interest in codes of conduct for transnational corporations and the general question of *Transfer of Technology*, including work done on this by an *ILO* committee. Brandt stresses the need for such a code to be of a nature, and implemented in such a way, that it does influence actual behaviour. The elements should include arrangements to ensure that agreement can be reached on conditions for direct investment that are of mutual benefit, and are then adhered to by the host countries and by the corporations: co-ordinated legislation on control of transnationals, including co-operation on tax policies to monitor transfer pricing; harmonization of the South's incentives to investment; and 'an international procedure for discussions and consultations on measures affecting direct investment and the activities of transnational corporations'(193), including the question of investment insurance to give greater confidence to investors.

Transport and Communications
Improvements in the transport and communications infrastructure are an essential basis for development in much of the South, especially in poorer land-locked countries. The Conference on International Economic Co-operation, 1975–77, noted a particular need in Africa and supported the call of the *Economic Commission for Africa* for an *African Transport and Communications Decade*.

Trees
see *Deforestation* and *Firewood*

UNCTAD – UN Conference on Trade and Development
The first UN Conference on Trade and Development was held in 1964 when the *Group of 77* was formed. Conferences meet about every four years, with a Trade and Development Board, a Special Committee on Preferences and standing committees for the continuing work. There is a secretariat in Geneva, which is a major centre for research into trade and development matters.

The 1964 Conference was mainly concerned with *Aid*, establishing the 'one per cent' target. This was refined at the 1968 Conference, which also established the *Generalized System of Preferences* for exports of manufactures from the South. 1972 concentrated on *Commodities*, leading to the introduction in 1976 of the plan for an *Integrated Programme for Commodities* centred on a *Common Fund*. The proposal for the Programme 'achieved partial agreement' at the 1979 Conference, 'which some regarded as a negotiating gain, others as a false start' (44).

Unemployment

Unemployment is a particularly acute problem for the countries of the South, because of their higher *Population Growth*. Total Third World unemployment and underemployment (it is difficult to draw the line between the two in the South) runs to hundreds of millions. In India alone, 8 million jobs must be created annually until the year 2000. Brandt (34) emphasizes that growing unemployment in the North must not become an excuse for not tackling the far greater jobs problem of the South. The *Mutual Interests* of North and South demand *Restructuring of Industry* in the North, so that growth and job creation can be sustained everywhere.

United Nations

The UN is the international organisation where the nations of the South outnumber and can outvote the nations of the North, whereas in the *International Monetary Fund* and *World Bank*, where voting strength is financially weighted, the North can outvote the South. The UN has therefore become 'the principal forum for the South' (37), stressing development needs and 'issues of international poverty'.

As 'the interplay of economic and political relations in today's world gives rise to a much more complex interdependence' (258), the role of the UN must be developed. But Brandt also argues the need for the UN and its associated organisations to become more effective. The tendency to found new institutions instead of facing problems direct has led to proliferation and overlapping. Brandt notes the burden of 'the very large number of international meetings – about 6000 every year in New York and Geneva; and the connected documentation – about a million pages a year' (260).

The UN has sought improvements, including the appointment, as recommended by an Expert Group, of a Director-General for Development and International Economic Cooperation. Brandt supports, as a further step, the 1968 proposal to the UN Committee for Development Planning for an advisory body to improve the effectiveness of the work of international institutions engaged in development and international co-operation. The members would be one-third from the South, one-third from the North and one-third 'selected for their experience and independent judgement'.

To ensure a balance of regional and other interests, the UN evolved first informally, and later as part of the constitution of UNCTAD, a system where member countries are divided into four Groups, amongst whom representation is distributed. They are Group A – African and Asian countries and Yugoslavia; Group B – Western European and non-European industrialized countries; Group C – Central and South American countries; Group D – Eastern European countries (China is outside the system). Groups A and C constitute the *Group of 77*. Brandt 'fully recognizes the validity and value' of the Group system, but notes that it has been criticized 'as tending to crystallize extreme positions on either side', and urges that North-South negotiations 'should look for joint gains rather than slowly wresting uncertain "concessions"'. The emphasis must be more on *Mutual Interests*. To achieve more effective negotiations, 'on each separate issues, such as commodities or trade, each group should nominate a limited number of countries most seriously interested in that issue' to the negotiating team (262).

Brandt wishes the UN to move away from a position where 'deliberations have often ended in resolutions which exhort everyone, without binding or committing any of the parties; the differences are drafted away to create an appearance of agreement, but they persist in reality. One result of this process is that the language of international resolutions has become inbred, specialized and coded' (262).

The principal UN agencies and other organizations concerned with development are:

Economic Commission for Africa
Economic Commission for Latin America
Economic and Social Commission for Asia and the Pacific
FAO – Food and Agriculture Organization
ILO – International Labour Organization
UN Centre on Transnational Corporations
UNCTAD
UN Development Programme
UNESCO
UN Fund for Population Activities
UN Group of Governmental Experts on the Relationship between Disarmament and Development

UN High Commission for Refugees
UN Industrial Development Organization and Fund
UN Institute for Training and Research
UN Revolving Fund for Natural Resources Exploitation
World Health Organization

Relevant UN Conferences and Activities are:

Charter of Economic Rights and Duties of States
Comprehensive New Programme of Action for the Least Developed Countries
Decade for Drinking Water and Sanitation
UN Conference on Science and Technology for Development
UN Conference on Technical Co-operation Amongst Developing Countries
UN Law of the Sea Conference
World Food Conference
Year of the Child

UN Centre (and Commission) on Transnational Corporations

The Centre on Transnational Corporations is an autonomous body within the UN Secretariat, serving the Commission on Transnational Corporations, a subsidiary of the UN Economic and Social Council. Its role is 'to further the understanding of the nature of transnational corporations and of their political, legal, economic and social effects on home and host countries and in international relations, particularly between developed and developing countries; to secure effective international arrangements aimed at enhancing the contribution of transnational corporations to national development goals and world economic strength while controlling and eliminating their negative effects; and to strengthen the negotiating capacity of host countries, in particular the developing countries, in their dealings with transnational corporations'.

Work on the Code of Conduct for Transnational Corporations was scheduled to be completed for the seventh session of the Commission in May 1981. The Code of Conduct is intended particularly to assist fulfillment of the aims of the *New International Economic Order*. Work is also in hand on international standards of company accounting and reporting.

UN Conference on Science and Technology for Development

This Conference proposed in 1979 that by the year 2000, 20 per cent of the world's research and development should take place in the South (3 per cent at present). An interim fund of $250 million was proposed for 1980–81, pending completion of a study for financing scientific and technological work in support of development.

UN Conference on Technical Co-operation Amongst Developing Countries

This Conference in 1978 identified areas where countries of the South should develop *Technical Co-operation* amongst themselves.

UN Development Programme

In 1966 the UN Special Fund and the Expanded Programme of Technical Assistance were merged under this new title, to assist by research, training, etc. (but not with development capital) in programmes of *Technical Co-operation*.

UNESCO – United Nations Educational Scientific and Cultural Organisation

UNESCO, set up in 1946, promotes international collaboration through education, science and culture. Its work is particularly aimed towards development problems, including the raising of levels of *Literacy*. Headquarters are in Paris.

UN Fund for Population Activities

Set up in 1967, it is responsible for matters relating to *Population Growth* and its relationships to economic and social development. Among other activities, it supports family planning programmes.

UN Group of Governmental Experts on the Relationship Between Disarmament and Development

This Group's work was planned over a three-year programme beginning in 1978. Its report is expected to reinforce the points made by Brandt about *Arms Spending* and development.

UN High Commission for Refugees
Set up in 1951 as a successor to the International Refugee Organization to provide protection and assistance to *Refugees and Displaced Persons*.

UNICEF – United Nations Children's Fund
One of the original UN agencies, with headquarters in New York, UNICEF aids programmes for child health, maternal and child nutrition and *Education*.

UN Industrial Development Organization and Fund (UNIDO)
Set up in 1967, with headquarters in Vienna, governed by the Industrial Development Board, to promote the industrialization of developing countries, including *Technical Co-operation* work for the *UN Development Programme*. The Fund was established in 1976, to enhance the ability of UNIDO to meet promptly and flexibly the needs of developing countries.

UN Institute for Training and Research
Set up in 1965, primarily to train people, especially from developing countries, for work in the UN and its agencies.

UN Law of the Sea Conference
This continuing Conference is particularly concerned with *Ocean Exploitation*, and with the proposal for an international *Sea-bed Authority*.

UN Revolving Fund for Natural Resources Exploitation
The Fund was set up in 1975 to encourage *Minerals* exploration, on the basis that the proceeds of successful exploration are used to cover the costs of unsuccessful ventures. Brandt maintains 'such an expectation is unreasonable for poor countries' owing to the Fund's repayment terms being too severe. They should be relaxed and 'the risks of financing spread over a far wider circle of countries interested in future mineral supplies'(157).

Water Supplies and Sanitation
Safe water supplies and proper sanitation are vital to health. 'Four out of five people living in rural areas of developing countries do not have reasonable access to even relatively un-

polluted water'(55). Fetching water is a heavy burden on women in these areas. Poor sanitation causes water-borne diseases particularly affecting children. 7 or 8 million children die each year in the South from diarrhoea caught from polluted water.

The UN Water Conference in 1977 declared the 1980s to be the *Decade for Drinking Water and Sanitation*, with the goal of safe drinking water and hygienic conditions for all by 1990. This means that 'the current rate of investment must be almost doubled in towns and increased fourfold in rural areas ... typical costs for simple standpipes or wells can be roughly estimated at 10 dollars per person for water in rural areas; the cost for house connections rise to $75 in rural areas and twice that in urban areas. For sanitation, typical costs are $5 per person in rural areas and $15 to $200 in towns, depending on whether sewerage is included'(56).

West African Development Bank
see *Regional Development Banks*

Women
The UN Decade for Women (1976–1985), stressing equality, development and peace, is now half over. Its aims and those of the World Conference on Women, 1980, which was particularly concerned with employment, health and education are of special relevance to the problems of women in the South.

Some aspects of the development process have direct effects on women. In much of the south alternative fuels to *Firewood* and better supplies of *Water* would lessen women's daily domestic burdens. *Food Production*, especially in Africa, is often a primary role for women. Brandt commends the 'FAO and World Bank guidelines on how to include women in their programmes'(60).

Health improvements are particularly needed for women – in the poorest countries women's life expectancy is lower than men's, not higher as in the North. In the attempt to limit *Population Growth* women are often more in favour of family planning than men.

At the same time, much development actually worsens the position of women. In the South, women's work is often in the *Informal Sector of the Economy*. Industrialization tends to leave women excluded from the money economy. Because their economic role is 'statistically invisible', this consequence is not measured by development assessments.

Brandt notes the analogy between the relationship of women to men and the 'unequal exchange' between North and South, and urges that 'any definition of development is incomplete if it fails to comprehend the contribution of women to development and the consequences of development for the lives of women'(59).

World Bank

The 'World Bank' is the name commonly used for the International Bank for Reconstruction and Development, one of the 1944 *Bretton Woods* institutions. The short name is misleading if it is understood as meaning that the Bank is in any sense a world central bank. The nearest approach to that is in fact the *IMF*. The long title of the Bank better describes what it is. The 'Reconstruction' aspect was concerned with war-devastated economies. The Bank is now the principal international development lending institution, and also, as a result, a centre for expertise and research on development matters.

134 countries, who have to be members of the IMF, are members of the Bank. Each makes a subscription according to its economic importance, on the same formula as that used for IMF subscriptions, and voting power is also the same as at the IMF, with the industrialized countries dominating. As well as using the subscription money (now $80 billion) the Bank borrows on world markets. This means that the loans it makes for development purposes are nearly at commercial rates of interest, but borrowers benefit from the fact that the Bank's credit standing is better than they can command. Loans are repayable over a period of twenty years or less, generally with a 'grace period' of five years. 34 per cent of the Bank's lending in the fiscal year 1980 was to countries with annual GNP per capita of $625 or less in 1978. 1980 lending commitments totalled $7 644m. in support of 144 projects in 48 countries. Loans on concessional terms ('soft loans') are made to the poorest countries by a subsidiary of the Bank, the *International Development Association*, which committed $3 838m. in 1980. Industrial loans are made by another subsidiary, the *International Finance Corporation* – $681m. in 1980.

Brandt believes that the Bank could, without damaging its credit rating, move from its present gearing ratio of 1 : 1, whereby its total borrowings cannot exceed its capitalization, to a ratio of 2 : 1 or more. Changes are also proposed in the structure and operations. 'A problem in the eyes of some is whether the World Bank is not too big and too concentrated: at present it has a professional staff of 2 400 of which over 95 per cent work in its headquarters in Washington. This concentration may help to achieve a unified approach, but it tends to make the staff more remote from the problems and attitudes in borrowing countries ... As the Bank acquires extra funds, it will grow further, making it all the more necessary to locate a larger part of its operational staff in regional centres in the different continents. This should also enable the Bank to attract and retain a wider range of staff from developing countries ... We recognize that nationality does not necessarily imply any particular bias ... but adequate representation of developing countries in staff and management, consistent with objective standards of quality in recruitment, will be an important step in building confidence'(248).

World Conference on Agrarian Reform and Rural Development

This 1979 Conference produced a Programme of Action intended to 'help countries integrate *Agricultural Development* and *Agrarian Reform* with overall development'.

World Development Fund

Brandt says that 'the creation of a new institution, which might be called a World Development Fund, has played a major role in the Commission's discussions ... a large share of the unmet needs, in particular a substantial level of programme loans' (see *Project Lending* v. *Programme Lending*), 'support for trade between middle-level and less-developed developing countries, and the financing of mineral exploration ... can be met by such an institution'. Brandt stresses that 'it is not our intention to suggest an institution that will overlap, much less work at cross-purposes, with existing ones: rather it is intended to complement and complete the existing structure'(252).

It is in particular envisaged that the Fund would have a more universal membership than existing institutions, with a more equal relationship between members, instead of the weighted voting that gives a dominance to the North in the *IMF* and *World Bank*. And 'the logic of a new system of universal and automatic revenues for world development points towards an institution ... which can serve as a channel for such revenues'(253).

World Food Conference
This Conference met in 1974, following the world food supply crisis in 1972–73. It called for international food security through international agreements.

World Health Organization – WHO
One of the original UN (and, earlier, League of Nations) specialized agencies, with headquarters in Geneva. Its task is to help control disease and improve general standards of health and nutrition through international co-operation. Most of the work has concentrated on the South. Total 1980–81 WHO budget is $427m.

World Intellectual Property Organization
This body is concerned together with *UNCTAD* with matters of *Patents*.

Year of the Child
In 1976 the UN General Assembly, 'recognizing the fundamental importance in all countries, developing and industrialized, of programmes benefiting children not only for the well-being of the children, but also as part of broader efforts to accelerate economic and social progress', declared that 1979 was to be the International Year of the Child. The aims were:

'(a) To provide a framework for advocacy on behalf of children and for enhancing the awareness of the special needs of children on the part of decision-takers and the public;
(b) To promote recognition of the fact that programmes for children should be an integral part of economic and social development plans with a view to achieving, in both the long term and the short term, sustained activities for the benefit of children at the national and international levels.'

A–Z Country Entries

Afghanistan

Population:	17m.
GNP per capita:	$125
Growth rate per capita:	1.7%
Development assistance per capita:	$3.19
Literacy rate:	less than 10%
International affiliations:	UN, Group of 77, Colombo Plan, ADB, IBRD
Defence Expenditure:	n/a

A dry, mountainous, central-Asian state. Most of the predominantly Muslim population is rural, living in tribes and clans and engaging in subsistence agriculture in the fertile plains and valleys which form 15% of the country. Fruit and bread form the staple diet, supplemented by meat, notably mutton. Since 1978 attempts to develop agriculture have involved land reform, the establishment of co-operatives and state farms and the introduction of fertilizer and equipment. Afghanistan is almost self-sufficient in food but imports sugar, tea, and some wheat. Much activity is outside the cash economy. The well-known sheepskins, cotton and fruit are the main agricultural exports. The capital, Kabul, is also the industrial centre with a number of small factories turning out cotton and woollen textiles, boots, furniture, glass and even pre-fabricated houses. Kandahar has a few large textile mills and fruit-canning plants. The main towns benefit from hydro-electric schemes. Natural gas from the north is exported to the Soviet Union. Mineral resources, including rich deposits of iron ore, are largely unexploited because they are inaccessible. Until recently, trade routes were evenly divided between Pakistan and the Soviet Union, with the latter as major partner for exports and imports. Main imports are petroleum products and textiles. There are no railways but there are 2 500 km of paved roads. With the help of UNESCO free elementary education has been growing although secondary education is limited to large towns. No reliable information is available on the economic effects of the Russian invasion.

Algeria

Population:	18m.
GNP per capita:	$954
Growth rate per capita:	2.1%

Development assistance per capita:	$7.58
Literacy rate:	26%
International affiliations:	UN, OAU, Arab League, OPEC, OAPEC, IAEA, Group of 77, N/A
Defence expenditure:	$705m.

A former French colony, independent since 1962, on the north coast of Africa. 95% of the population lives on 12% of the land, between the Mediterranean coast and the Saharan mountains. There is migration to Algiers, the capital, and other towns in this area. Most of the fertile land is controlled by self-management committees, growing wheat, barley, wine, olive oil and dates. With present population growth, wheat imports are necessary. The rest of the country to the south consists of mountains, desert and steppe. In the mountain region, where access is difficult, the poor population live by grazing cattle, sheep, goats and camels. On the coast, sardines and anchovies are fished. In total, agriculture employs 60% of the labour force and accounts for less than 10% of GDP. 92% of export earnings come from oil and oil products. Algeria is the thirteenth-largest oil producer in the world and its gas reserves are the fourth-largest. Industry employing 11% of the work-force has developed on this basis, concentrated in petro-chemicals, plastics and fertilizers as well as iron and steel. The state controls nearly all industry, with a fixed maximum percentage for foreign investment. Over-ambitious expansion in the early 1970s led to fiscal conservatism in the mid-1970s. The EEC and the USA are the main export and import partners, with France as the leading supplier. Imports consist of capital goods, consumer goods, food, drink and tobacco and are restricted by the government. There are 18 600 km of roads, 3 800 km railways and 65 government airfields. 57% of school-age children attended school in 1970; there are four universities including Algiers which has over 60 000 students. There is a preventive medicine programme.

Angola

Population:	7m.
GDP per capita:	$434
Growth rate per capita:	− 2.7%

Development assistance per capita:	$2.56
Literacy rate:	15–20%
International affiliations:	OAU, Group of 77, N/A
Defence expenditure:	(32 500 men)

Angola, a former Portuguese colony, lies on the south-west coast of Africa, north of Namibia and south and west of Zaire and the Congo. The population is concentrated in the north and west and is ethnically mixed (40% Ovimbundu, 23% Kimbundu). The dominant group are the *mestiços* (mixed African and European descent) who form 1–2%. The narrow, 1 600 km-long coastal strip is flat and semi-arid. The main ports are Luanda (the capital) and Lobito. The land rises abruptly inland to a large plateau. The country is dry in the south all year and in the north is dry from May to October but hot and humid the rest of the year. Coffee, cotton and sisal are grown for export, maize and other crops for food. Cattle, sheep, goats and pigs are kept. 80% of the work force is in agriculture which occupies 22% of the land. There is a small amount of light industry and cement production, mostly nationalized. The economy is still recovering from the civil war in 1975 and the subsequent guerrilla fighting. Cabinda offshore oil is the mainstay of the economy, bringing in 70% of export earnings. Diamonds are also exported. Angola relies on imports for transport equipment and textiles and to make up its food deficit, but lack of money has forced a cut-back. The USA and Portugal are the main export partners; Portugal and West Germany are the main suppliers. The Benguela railway was an important source of revenue from Zaire and Zambia before the civil war and has now been repaired. There are 72 000 km of mainly unpaved roads. In 1977 there were over a million pupils at school and 1 100 at university.

Argentina

Population:	26.1m.
GDP per capita:	$1 934
Growth rate per capita:	1.0%
Development assistance per capita:	$1.07
Literacy rate:	more than 90%
International affiliations:	UN, LAFTA, OAS, Group of 77, N/A

Defence expenditure: $2.8bn.

Argentina is the major part of the South American continent, south of the Tropic of Capricorn to Cape Horn and west from the South Atlantic to the Andes (the frontier with Chile). 97% of the population is of European descent, 72% is urban and 33% live in the capital, Buenos Aires. The northern part of the country is sub-tropical lowland, the western part the Andes mountains and the south, the Patagonian steppe, but the wealth of Argentina derives from the temperate pampas in the east and centre. In this area, mainly on large, private estates, cattle and sheep are raised. In 1978 there were 61.3 million cattle (more than double the population) and 34 million sheep producing 10% of the world's wool. On average, Argentinians consume 115kg of red meat each year; the rest is exported. Wheat is the third agricultural export. Other products include oilseeds, cotton, potatoes, tobacco and fruit and olive trees. Wine-growing is centred around Mendoza in the west. Agriculture employs 19% of the work-force and industry 25%. Industrial activities are food processing, motor vehicle manufacturing, consumer goods, textiles, chemicals, printing and metal production. Membership of trade unions was 2.5 million in 1976. Argentina is also rich in natural resources (notably lead, zinc, tin, copper, iron, gold, silver, manganese), and produces electrical equipment, wood, newsprint, crude oil, automative equipment, iron and steel products and chemicals. Main suppliers are the EEC, the USA and LAFTA partners. The EEC takes 33% of Argentina's exports and the USA is the next biggest consumer. In 1976, there were 309 000 km of highway and 37 000 km of railway. There were more than 50 newspapers and 10 TV stations. Free medical attention is available in public hospitals. There is free, compulsory education up to the age of 14 and there are 10 universities, including those at Buenos Aires and Cordoba.

Bangladesh

Population:	87m.
GDP:	$9.5bn.
Growth rate per capita:	− 0.4%
Development assistance per capita:	$8.77
Literacy rate:	23%
International affiliations:	UN, Colombo Plan

Defence expenditure: $115m.

Formally the eastern province of Pakistan, Bangladesh declared independence after the civil war of 1971. Situated to the north of the Bay of Bengal, the country is bordered by India to the north and west and by Burma to the east. Agriculture accounts for some 50% of the GDP and employs some 80% of the working population. Rice growing dominates over 80% of the agricultural land. The Ganges delta provides much of the energy supply through hydro-systems and also much of the water supply for agriculture. Thus the main areas of Government investment have been in agriculture, irrigation, flood control, and rural development. The delta area has also provided Bangladesh with a valuable system of navigable water for cheap transportation. It has also provided access to a substantial fishery which is an important source of food. There are over 4 000 km of railway, and over 5 000 km of paved roads. There is central Government control of the education system, over 40 000 primary schools, and 8 000 secondary schools. In further education there are 6 universities, 22 polytechnics, 6 teacher training establishments, and 48 primary teacher training colleges. There are over 14 000 hospital beds. 80% of the population is Muslim and there are close contacts with most of the other Muslim nations.

Crops: Rice, jute, sugar-cane, wheat, tobacco, tea.
Minerals: Coal, limestone, white clay, glass sand
Exports: Jute, hides, leather, tea
Imports: Machinery, transport equipment, food grains, mineral fuels, chemicals, drugs, and consumer goods.
Trade partners: UK, EEC, Pakistan, India, SE Asia and China

Botswana

Population:	816 000
GNP:	$470m.
Growth rate per capita:	13.3%
Development assistance per capita:	$69.86
Literacy rate:	20%
International affiliations:	UN, OAU, CW, ACP
Defence expenditure:	(2 000 armed men)

Formerly the Bechuanaland Protectorate, Botswana gained

independence from Britain in 1966, and is a republic. It comprises the territory lying between the Molopo River to the south and the Zambezi to the north, and extending from the Transvaal Province (South Africa) and Zimbabwe on the east to Namibia on the west. The climate is mainly subtropical and dry throughout the year. Nearly 70% of the population are engaged in agriculture, and over 12% are employed outside Botswana, mainly in mining in South Africa. Cattle raising and dairying are the principal occupations, while the principal source of foreign earnings are diamonds, nickel-copper, and meat exports. Botswana's capital is Gaborone.

Natural resources: Minerals, including diamonds, nickel-copper, copper, salt, and soda-ash
Agriculture: Crops are dependent on the rainfall, cattle-rearing and dairying being the main occupations. Reforms in land ownership in 1975 have contributed to more modern land use.
Animals: The abattoir at Lobatse is of great importance to the country's economy. In 1978 there were 3m. cattle, 1.15m. goats, 440 000 sheep, 600 000 poultry.
Industries: Food-processing and mining
Exports: Diamonds, meat products, copper, nickel
Imports: Food and beverages, tobacco, machinery and electrical equipment, textiles and footwear, fuels, vehicles, metal and metal products
Communications: 15 000 km of roads, 19 000 vehicles; 640 km of railway; three airports
Education: 336 primary schools, 15 secondary, 15 government-aided, 14 private secondary, 26 vocational training, 3 teacher-training colleges; University of Botswana and Swaziland – *c.* 1750 students

Brazil

Population:	126m.
GDP:	$201bn.
Growth rate per capita:	6.2%
Development assistance per capita:	$1.09
Literacy rate:	60%
International affiliations:	UN, OAS, LAFTA
Defence expenditure:	$2.09bn.

Brazil is the largest country on the South American continent, both in population and land mass. It has an extensive coastline bordering the Atlantic, and has boundaries with all the South American countries except Chile and Ecuador. Over 40% of the population is engaged in agriculture, and 75% of foreign exchange derives from agricultural exports. Brazil is more than self-sufficient in food and agricultural products, and these provide a secure basis for the manufacturing industry of the country. Processing of food products employs nearly 12% of the working population. Coffee is the most important cash crop in the country as well as being the largest single export earner. Brazil also has major fishing and timber industries: the fishing catch in 1979 was 750 000 tons, while its pulp industry is the largest in South America. Brazil is also rich in minerals, being the world's largest source for quartz crystal and the second-largest source of chrome. A large area of the country's land surface is covered in forest, whilst abundant supplies of water form a major basis for its hydro-electric power and transport system. Production of electricity exceeds consumption. Brazil's two major cities are Rio de Janeiro (pop. 4.5m.) and Sao Paulo (pop. 8m.).

Natural resources: quartz crystal, diamonds, mica, chrome, manganese, tungsten, coal
Crops: Coffee, rubber, cocoa, timber, wheat, oranges, bananas, wool, rice, tobacco
Animals: Cattle, sheep, pigs, goats, poultry
Industry: Food-processing, chemicals, metallurgy, transport equipment, textiles, hydro-electric power
Exports: Coffee, machinery, soybeans, iron ore
Imports: Crude petroleum, machinery, wheat, fertilizers, coal
Trading partners: USA, Germany, Netherlands, Japan, France, U.K., Italy, Argentina
Communications: 1.5m. km of highways, 9m. vehicles. Two railway systems: Federal – 23 500 km; Sao Paulo State Railway – 5 000 km. Good aircraft links and over 35 000 km of navigable inland waterway. Rio de Janeiro and Santos are the principal ports.

Burma
Population:	34m.
GNP:	$9.5bn.
Growth rate per capita:	1.8%

Development assistance per capita:	$2.47
Literacy rate:	70%
International affiliations:	UN, Colombo Plan, IMF, GATT, Group of 77, N/A
Defence expenditure:	$115.4m.

The socialist republic of Burma is on the eastern side of the Bay of Bengal with India to the west and China and Siam to the East. A tongue of territory stretches down the Malay peninsula. The population is predominantly rural. 72% are Burmans and the remainder are Karens, Shan, Indian and Chinese minorities. The climate is tropical monsoon with up to 200 inches of rain annually. In the north-west and north-east there are mountain ranges rising to 15 000 feet. The main crops are rice, sugar-cane, maize and groundnuts. Cotton, sugar-cane and jute have been the subject of development programmes to increase quality and quantity. Agriculture accounts for 27% of GDP and 75% of exports. The main animals reared are cattle and buffalo, used for ploughing. The government-controlled forests produce hardwood, fire-wood and bamboo, with the help of 2 780 working elephants. Burma provides 76% of the world's teak. Industry produces foodstuffs, textiles, footwear, timber products and petrol, but rates of growth fell back in the mid-1970s. Lead, zinc, tungsten and oil are extracted but have not met the targets of the Third 4th-year plan (1978/9–1982/3). In the 1960s, the government nationalized banks, commerce, oil and other sectors. There are more than 35 000 co-operatives and over 15 000 state factories. Burma exports rice and teak to India, Western Europe, China and Japan; and imports machinery, transport equipment, textiles and manufactured goods, mainly from Japan and Western Europe. There are 8 years compulsory education, but attendance is only 40%. There are 33 000 km of road and 140 km of canal, but the lifeline of Burma is the Irrawaddy River, navigable up to 1 440 km inland, and the Irrawaddy delta's 3 200 km of waterway.

Burundi

Population:	4.38m.
GDP:	$706m.
Growth rate per capita:	0.8%

Development assistance
per capita: $12.59
Literacy rate: 9%
International affiliations: UN, OAU, ACP
Defence expenditure: $22m.

Burundi is situated between Tanzania and Zaire and borders
with Rwanda to the North. It has no direct access to the sea.
The main communications routes are by road through Rwanda
and Uganda, or by ship down Lake Tanganyika to the
Tanzania railways. Burundi has been independent since 1962.
It is one of the most densely populated countries in Africa,
with over 147 persons per square kilometre. Over 85% of the
population are reliant on subsistence agriculture. Coffee is the
main cash crop and accounts for 80% of state revenue and 90%
of exports. The country depends heavily on international aid
for its capital programme. There have been considerable efforts to reduce the dependence on coffee as a major source of
income, and an increasing emphasis on tea cultivation: in three
years there has been a 73% increase in its cultivation with a
present area of 4 600 hectares under cultivation. Rice growing
is also gaining in importance. Burundi has substantial deposits
of gold, nickel, and uranium as well as traces of oil, although
at present the country lacks the infrastructure to enable it to
exploit these reserves.

Crops: Coffee, tea, cassava, potatoes, bananas, beans, maize
and rice
Animals: Ankole cattle, goats, sheep
Agriculture: 85% work-force, 40% land
Industry: Food-processing, construction, some consumer
goods
Exports: Coffee, tea, some minerals
Imports: Textiles, food, machinery, petroleum products.
Partners: Belgium, France, West Germany, Japan, Kenya
Education: 32% primary school attendance

Cameroon
Population: 8.4m.
GNP: $3 180m.
Growth rate per capita: 1.3%
Development assistance
per capita: $53.27

Literacy rate:	65%
International affiliations:	UN, OAU, ACP, Group of 77, N/A
Defence expenditure:	$72.9m.

The United Republic of Cameroon is a union of former French and British territory, situated on the Gulf of Guinea in the 'armpit' of West Africa, a few degrees north of the Equator. Inland from the coastal rain-forest, there is a plateau reaching 1 350m. The western part of the country is forested and mountainous, and the northern is savanna. Temperatures are high; the coast is very humid and the north very dry. Cocoa and coffee form 60% of exports. Bananas, plantains, maize, cotton and rubber are also grown. In the north and centre cattle, sheep and goats are reared. Altogether agriculture occupies 35% of the land and 75% of the people. Cash-crops account for 70% of exports; the diversity of crops offers some protection against unstable prices. The government provides credit, fertilizer, insecticides and marketing. 15% of the labour force works in industry producing 14% of GNP in the shape of shoes, soap, oil products, foodstuffs and aluminium. The main natural resources are timber, oil, and bauxite. At Edea there is an aluminium complex powered by hydro-electricity, processing ore from Guinea. Cameroon's main trading partners are France, the rest of Western Europe and the USA. Manufactured consumer goods, capital goods, food and fuel are imported. The country has proved attractive to foreign investors, largely because of tax and duty exemptions. In 1976 there were one and a quarter million pupils of all ages; the education programme is extensive as reflected by the literacy figure for a country with 24 indigenous languages and two foreign, albeit official languages (French and English). There is a university at Yaoundé the capital. 80% of the population live in the Francophone east. Much of the country is inaccessible during the rainy season. Attempts to improve the infrastructure are hampered by transport difficulties. These may be alleviated when the Trans-Cameroonian railway is completed. The main port, Douala, is being expanded.

Central African Republic

Population:	1.69m.
GNP:	$535m.
Growth rate per capita:	0.8%

Development assistance	
per capita:	$16.18
Literacy rate:	18%
International affiliations:	UN, OAU, ACP, OCAM,
	UDEAC, Group of 77, N/A
Defence expenditure:	$13.5m.

Landlocked in the heart of Africa, 5° north of the Equator, the CAR was formerly part of Equatorial Africa, and for four years, until 1979, was an Empire under Bokassa. The country is vulnerable to changes in weather and suffers from shortages of investment, infrastructure and trained personnel. The CAR depends heavily on foreign oil and is very undeveloped. The country is formed by a large well-watered, wooded plateau, merging into rain-forest in the south-west and semi-desert on the north-east. Average temperature reaches 90°F; rain, mostly from June to November, measures 175cm annually. Coffee and cotton form 40% of exports and diamonds and timber contribute the same amount. The population is 70% rural. The other crops are sorghum, maize and groundnuts. Cattle and goats are reared. However, agricultural activity is only carried out on 10% of the land. There is a small amount of industrial production, processing agricultural goods. France is the main trading partner. The CAR imports machinery, motor vehicles, cotton textiles and petroleum products. There are 216 000 primary school pupils and over 20 000 students at secondary and tertiary levels including the University of Bangui, the capital city. There is a hydro-electric scheme at Mpoko Falls. The total lack of railways will be remedied by the planned new route from Bangui to connect up with the Trans-Cameroonian railway.

Chad

Population:	4.49m.
GNP:	$945m.
Growth rate per capita:	− 0.9%
Development assistance	
per capita:	$15.98
Literacy rate:	7%
International affiliations:	UN, OAU, ACP, GATT,
	OCAM, AFDB
Defence expenditure:	$22.2m.

Chad lies in the centre of North Africa, with the Sudan to the east, Libya to the north and the CAR to the south. Chad, the traditional crossroads of desert Muslims and rain-forest inhabitants, is extremely undeveloped. The country is isolated and landlocked with a large northern desert and poor soil elsewhere, a dry climate, scarce mineral resources, famine and drought. Attempts to improve conditions have been undermined by civil war since February 1979. Subsistence agriculture accounts for half of GNP. Cotton is the main cash crop and forms 80% of exports. Date production is increasing. Cattle, sheep and goats form a major resource; meat is the second largest export and until 1967 Chad was self-sufficient in food. Between 1967 and 1973 many people and animals died in a major drought. 90% of the working population is in agriculture. Fishing in rivers and Lake Chad supplies the domestic market, and smoked fish are exported to Nigeria. Industry employs 4% of the work-force processing livestock products and textiles and assembling bicycles and radios. Trade figures are unreliable because of the open frontier with Nigeria, which is officially the second trading partner after the EEC. Chad imports petroleum products, textile yarn, sugar, machinery, food, motor vehicles and construction materials. There were 247 000 children at school and 800 students at the University of N'djamena in 1977. Of the 31 000 kilometres of road, only 240 km are paved.

Chile

Population:	11.2m.
GNP:	$15bn.
Growth rate per capita:	0.2%
Development assistance per capita:	$4.63
Literacy rate:	n/a
International affiliations:	UN, OAS, LAFTA, Group of 77
Defence expenditure:	$726m.

Chile runs for 4 240 km down the west coast of South America, squeezed into a 192 km wide strip of land between the Andes and the Pacific. The north is desert; the centre, which includes the capital Santiago, is the agricultural zone with a Mediterranean climate; the south is an area of forests and pasture and the extreme south is barren land with fjords and islets except for some rich pampa on the Atlantic side. Chile has been independent since 1818. State-directed industrial development has been going on since the late 1930s, but Chile's wealth has been based on minerals. Chile grows cereals and fruit and cattle, sheep, goats and horses are reared in the south and central regions. Livestock accounts for 52% of agricultural output. Chilean agriculture has developed greatly and there is scope for further growth; the country once imported two-thirds of its food and now only 12%. Chile's forests contribute pine, eucalyptus and poplar; timber, paper and pulp are exported. Fish and fish products are also exported. The main export (48% of total) is copper, which provides 30% of government revenue and 40% of world production. Chile also has iron ore, oil and gas in the south, sodium nitrate, coal in the north, molybdenum, manganese, lead and zinc. There are state-owned copper and steel plants. Chile has two experimental British nuclear reactors and plans to build a nuclear power station. Main trading partners are the USA, Germany, Japan and Brazil. Chile imports fuels, chemicals, industrial and transport equipment, live animals and food. The present government is fiscally conservative, has removed price controls and encourages foreign investment and the private sector. There are 66 000 km of roads, half of them paved and 8 300 km of railway line. There are 8 years of free, compulsory education, 2 million primary schoolchildren and 8 universities with 96 000 students (1970).

China

Population:	1 025m.
GNP:	n/a
Growth rate per capita	n/a
Development assistance per capita:	n/a
Literacy rate:	n/a
International affiliations:	UN, IAEA, IBRD, IDA
Defence expenditure:	$40.6bn.(est.)

China is the third-largest country in the world with the biggest population and one of the oldest civilizations (c.1500 BC). Two-thirds of the country is mountain or semi-desert; 90% of the population lives on the fertile plains and deltas in the eastern sixth of the country. China has depended upon intensive agriculture for centuries and it remains the basis of the economy, employing 85% of the people. Most of the country has a temperate, monsoonal climate, hot and humid in summer with frequent floods and cool and dry in winter. Cereals, cotton, soybeans, tea and oilseeds are the main crops. China is the third-largest producer of pigmeat in the world; in 1978 there were 300 million pigs, 94 million cattle and 170 million sheep. The main forest products are teak and oil from the *dong* tree, mainly in Sichuan.

Since the establishment of the People's Republic in 1949 development policies have varied, especially during the Cultural Revolution after 1965. In 1958 there was 'The Great Leap Forward' designed to utilize the rural surplus labour by the establishment of decentralized communes and rural industry. In the 1960s more than 20 million people moved to the countryside; family and individual plots were introduced. China is now following a 10-year plan (1976–85) with the emphasis on mechanization of agriculture and centralized control. The long-term aim, formulated by Chou en-lai in 1975, is to become a first-class economic power by 2000 A.D., through the four modernizations: agriculture, industry, defence and science and technology. Industrial production, concentrated in iron and steel, coal, machinery, light industry and armaments, employs 95 million people and grew by 14% (1977–78) and 12% (1978–79). China exports agricultural goods, textiles, light-industry products, crude oil, iron and steel and imports grain, fertilizer, raw materials, machinery and equipment, minerals and metals. Main trading partners are Japan, Hong Kong, Germany, Roumania, France and Singapore. In a major reversal of policy in 1978 China began actively seeking foreign aid, credit and investment and above all technology. Her capacity to absorb imports was overestimated and original targets have been reduced. China lacks a comprehensive transport system but 83% of communes are accessible by road; there are 48 000 km of railway and a national transport network is planned on the basis of 136 000 km of waterway, which includes the Yangtze Kiang, the world's fourth-largest river. The big expansion in education was from 1949–59 when universal primary education was achieved. 5 years' education is compulsory but the average is higher. There are many universities including two in Peking. Chinese medicine has spread rapidly. There are 2½ million professional medical workers including 770 000 western-style doctors, 250 000 Chinese doctors and 1 600 000 'barefoot doctors'.

Colombia

Population:	26.52m.
GNP:	$14.5bn.
Growth rate per capita:	4.0%
Development assistance per capita:	$2.93
Literacy rate:	73%
International affiliations:	UN, OAS, IBRD, IDB, LAFTA, Andean Pact, ICO, Group of 77
Defence expenditure:	$215m.

Colombia has the fourth-largest population in South America and is situated on the north-east coast of the continent, adjacent to the isthmus of Panama. A flat tropical coastal zone fronts the Pacific and the Caribbean. The rest of the western part of the country is made up of three mountain ranges running NE–SE; this cool, well-watered region contains most of the cities. 64.3% of the population is urban and the majority of people live above 1 200 m. The eastern plains – 'Uaros' – occupy 54% of the land but contain less than 3% of the people. Agriculture employs 45% of the work-force on 20% of the land and produces 30% of GDP. In the coastal areas, bananas, rice, sugar-cane, plantains and tobacco are grown; in the highlands, the world's second-largest coffee crop is grown, bringing in 50% of Colombia's foreign exchange. Tropical hardwoods, pine and eucalyptus are harvested and rubber is now being cultivated but 150 million acres of forest in the east remain unexploited. The varying land elevation allows the country a wide range of crops and agriculture is growing faster than population. Industrial products are textiles, processed food, clothing, footwear, beverages, chemicals and metal products but the most dynamic sector is engineering. As well as coffee, Colombia exports clothing, chemicals and metals. Natural resources include oil, natural gas, iron ore, nickel, gold and copper and 90% of the world's emeralds. Imports are machinery, electrical equipment, chemical and metal products and transport equipment. Main trading partners: USA, Germany, Andean Pact. Oil was exported until 1976 but has been imported since then. The mountains inhibit good communication; 51 000 km roads, 2 912 km railways. Primary education is free but not compulsory nor is it always available. The national university is in Bogota, the capital, and there are many others.

Congo, The People's Republic of

Population:	1.525m.
GNP:	$877m.
Growth rate per capita:	0.1%
Development assistance per capita:	$42.73
Literacy rate:	20%
International affiliations:	UN, OAU, UDEAC, OCAM, ACP, Group of 77, N/A
Defence expenditure:	$37.2m.

The Congo is on the Equator in west central Africa forming a 'J' shape between Gabon and Zaire, with a short coastline at the bottom tip. The capital Brazzaville (across the river from Kinshasa, Zaire) lies in the fertile Nairi valley (the curve of the 'J'). North of this area is the central Bateke plateau, then impassable flood-plains and in the far north, dry savanna. The tropical climate produces an average temperature of 75°F and 112–200 cm of rain annually. Despite an increase in the urban population (50% of the total in 1979), 70% of the work-force live in isolated, rural communities growing subsistence crops – cereals, banana, cassava, rice, groundnuts, and fruits and rearing goats and chickens. There is a small quantity of cash crops, notably sugar-cane and tobacco, marketed by the state. The Congo depends heavily on imports, including 90% of meat consumed. Less than one per cent of the land is cultivated. There is only light industry processing agricultural and forest products. Services, transport and customs revenues are important sources of income derived from goods en route to surrounding countries. A dam is being built at D'Jaire to provide hydro-electricity for Brazzaville. The main exports are tropical woods, sugar and tobacco; imports – machinery, vehicles, consumer goods and food; main partners – France and Italy. There is a long-term trade deficit. The poor roads (only 350 km tarred) inhibit agricultural development and exploitation of the forest. The main railway runs from the capital to Pointe-Noire the main port. In 1974 there were nearly 400 000 children at school; there are 4 000 students at the University of Brazzaville.

Costa Rica

Population:	1.87m.
GNP:	n/a
Growth rate per capita:	3.3%
Development assistance per capita:	$13.28
Literacy rate:	n/a
International affiliations:	UN, OAS, IMF, IBRD, CACM, IDB, Rio Pact, Group of 77
Defence expenditure:	(5000 troops)

Costa Rica is a narrow strip of southern Central America between Nicaragua and Panama. The country was 'discovered' by Columbus and was a Spanish colony of poor independent smallholders for three centuries. After independence in 1821, first coffee and later bananas were introduced laying the agricultural basis for the economy which continues today. The land is mainly rugged hills and mountains with a wide eastern plain and a narrow western one. Two-thirds of the land is forested, notably with rosewood, cedar and mahogany but these woods are only partially exploited. Most people live in higher areas as lowland temperatures are in excess of 90°F. 35% of the work-force produces 2% of GDP from agriculture growing sugar and grains as well as the two big export crops, coffee and bananas. Honey is gathered and sold to the USA and 2 million cattle grazed providing beef for home population and export. 15% of the work-force is engaged in light industry processing foods, producing pharmaceuticals, drinks, wood products, chemicals and fertilizers. Tourism and construction also contribute to national income. Hydro-electric schemes in the mountains provide electricity. Imports are: transport equipment, machines, paper products, oil, electrical machinery and food. The main partners are the USA and the members of the Central American Common Market. Natural resources include small quantities of bauxite, sulphur, gold and oil. There are 9 500 km of all-weather roads and railways from San José, the central capital, to Limon, the Caribbean port and Puntareras, the Pacific port. Primary education is free and compulsory, secondary is free. The University of Costa Rica (founded 1843) has 24 000 students. There is social insurance and family assistance.

Cuba

Population:	9.9m.
GNP:	$12.6bn.
Growth rate per capita:	− 1.4%
Development assistance per capita:	$3.39
Literacy rate:	96%
International affiliations:	UN, Comecon, GATT, ISC, (OAS), IDB, Group of 77, N/A
Defence expenditure:	$1.1bn.

Cuba lies at the western end of the Greater Antilles islands which form the northern boundary of the Caribbean Sea. It is just inside the Tropic of Cancer, 144 km south of Key West, Florida. 60% of the land is composed of fertile valleys and plains and the rest is mountainous and hilly. Tradewinds produce a semi-tropical climate with average temperatures of 75°F; there are 135 cm of rain annually, most of which falls from May to October. Agricultural land, which is state-owned, occupies 65% of the total area and employs 34% of the work-force. The main crops remain those introduced by the Spanish and worked by black slaves: sugar and tobacco. Sugar and its by-products account for 20% of GDP and 86% of exports. The 1970 crop was a world record. Other crops are coffee, rice, beans, fruit and vegetables. Cattle, pig and poultry production is rising. Forests containing cedar, eucalyptus, mahogany, gums and resins now produce less than 10% of exports. Cuba imports nearly all its oil, a lot of food and 20% of consumer goods. It has a long-term trade deficit; 44% of export earnings are used for debt-servicing because high borrowing has been necessary to maintain high investment rates (20% GNP p.a.). Cuba would be very vulnerable to fluctuations in sugar prices on the open market but since 1959 the bulk of trade has switch-ed from the USA to the Communist Bloc which provides fixed-price sugar contracts. A highway and railway run the length of the island. Education is free and compulsory from ages 6–14. There were four universities with 40 000 students in 1978. Good quality medical services are free and widely available. Cuba has the lowest infant mortality in Latin America.

Dominican Republic

Population:	5.62m.
GNP:	$4.3bn.
Growth rate per capita:	4.3%
Development assistance per capita:	$6.67
Literacy rate:	70%
International affiliations:	UN, IBRD, IMF, GATT, IAEA, OAS, IADB, IBA, Group of 77
Defence expenditure:	$91m.

The Dominican Republic, an ex-Spanish colony, occupies the eastern two-thirds of the Caribbean island of Hispaniola, while the ex-French colony of Haiti occupies the western part. There are mountains in the north and centre with a fertile valley between them called the 'Cibao' where food is grown. The climate is maritime tropical moderated by the tradewinds: temperature 72–83°F, rain 137–150 cm. Hurricane David damaged three hydro-electric plants in 1979. Until recently agriculture was the main source of wealth. The country has been self-sufficient in rice since the 1930s and has been a net food exporter for many years. In particular, sugar, coffee, cacao and beef are exported. The government's aim is to diversify food production to make the Dominican Republic the 'granary of the Caribbean'. Industry employed 130 000 people in 1975 in sugar refining and the production of textiles, pharmaceuticals, cements and light manufactures. Industry developed rapidly in Free Trade Zones in the early 1970s but one of the highest growth rates in Latin America was halted by a drop in the world price for sugar coincidental with a large increase in oil prices. Natural resources include nickel, bauxite, silver and gold; in total minerals account for 22% of foreign earnings with ferro-nickel and bauxite as the main items. Foodstuffs, oil, industrial raw materials and capital goods are imported. The bulk of all trade is with the USA. Until 1964 there was generally a trading surplus but since then deficits have appeared. Roads provide the main transport network. There are 5 224 km of first-class roads, including four-lane concrete highways. There are 1 400 km of railways for sugar and 100 km for passengers. The main port is the capital, Santo Domingo. Education is free and compulsory from 7–14 but attendance is only 60%. There are 27 000 students at the

University of Santo Domingo. 78 towns have complete water-works systems.

Ecuador

Population:	7.9m.
GNP:	$7bn.
Growth rate per capita:	5.2%
Development assistance per capita:	$9.22
Literacy rate:	n/a
International affiliations:	UN, OAS, LAFTA, Andean Pact, OPEC, Group of 77
Defence expenditure:	$163m.

Ecuador is on the Equator on the north-west coast of South America with Colombia to the north and Peru to the south. The country falls into three regions. Firstly, on the coast between the Andes and the Pacific, about one quarter of the land area, bananas, coffee, cacao and sugar are grown for export; the climate here is hot and humid. Next is the Sierra, the highlands plateau from 2 400–3 000m above sea level where rice, maize, barley and potatoes are grown for domestic consumption. 60% of the population lives in this region which includes the capital, Quito, but migration to the coast is increasing. Temperatures vary from 50–70°F daily throughout the year. East of the Andes is half of the country, the 'Oriente', which is mainly tropical jungle. Amazon tribes are found in this region. The Galapagos islands with their strange fauna, 960 km off the coast, belong to Ecuador. The country's development has been hampered by political turmoil ever since independence in 1830. Sheep, cattle, and pigs are raised in the Sierra. In total, agriculture employs 56% of the work-force on 15% of the land. Ecuador has a growing fishing fleet with the biggest catch in tuna and shrimps for export. Industry produces foodstuffs, textiles and light consumer goods and has grown rapidly, now employing 18% of the work-force. The catalyst of development was the discovery of oil in the 'Oriente' in the 1960s. Even with oil, Ecuador remains one of the least developed countries in South America; income distribution is very uneven. The 1970s have been bedevilled by inflation. Ecuador imports industrial raw materials, machinery, transport equipment and wheat. Main partners are the USA, LAFTA and the EEC. Education is free and compulsory from 6 to 14. There

are 17 000 km of roads, many narrow and dangerous; 965 km
of railway and 7 ports. Ecuador is noted for its sport and culture, particularly the 'indigenismo' movement.

Egypt

Population:	40.46m.
GNP:	$16.5bn.
Growth rate per capita:	6.2%
Development assistance per capita:	$27.11
Literacy rate:	38%
International affiliations:	UN, Arab League, OAU, GATT, OAPEC, Group of 77, N/A
Defence expenditure:	$2.17bn.

Egypt forms the north-east corner of Africa with Libya to the
west, Sudan to the south, the Mediterranean to the north and
Israel and the Red Sea to the east. The country has a recorded
history of 5 000 years. Most of Egypt is rainless, uncultivable
desert. In the east are rugged hills and mountains. 50% of the
workforce are engaged in agriculture on 3% of the land, growing cotton, wheat, rice and maize mainly for market. The cultivable area is the Nile valley and delta and some oases. The
Aswan Dam and irrigation is extending this area. Agricultural
techniques are primitive but the soil is fertile. In 1947, 2% of
the people owned half the land but agrarian reform has fixed
a maximum of 100 acres per family. The law requires landowners to sow not less than a third of their land with wheat and
not more than a third with cotton. Nevertheless, wheat has to
be imported. Agricultural products, mainly cotton, account
for 80% of exports. The government has concentrated on
industrial development with most industry in the public sector. Products are textiles, processed food, tobacco, chemicals,
fertilizer, petroleum products. There are two uranium
processing plants. In total industry employs 11% of the work-
force and contributes more than 20% of GNP and 35% of
exports. Egypt suffers from a classic cycle of underdevelop-
ment: balance of payments problems lead to import restrictions which inhibit agricultural and industrial growth, which
reduces exports which exacerbates the balance of payments
problem. Egypt's role in the Middle East conflict has hampered continuous economic development. Education is free

from 6 to 12. There are four universities including one in Cairo, the capital. Railways: 6 400 km. Roads: 22 400 km. Waterways: Nile river system 1 600 km, canals 1 600 km.

El Salvador

Population:	4.71m.
GNP:	$3.05bn.
Growth rate per capita:	1.9%
Development assistance per capita:	$9.37
Literacy rate:	50%
International affiliations:	UN, OAS, ODECA, CACM
Defence expenditure:	$72m.

El Salvador is a small Central American country with a south-facing Pacific coast. To the north is Honduras, to the east Nicaragua and to the west Guatemala. The land is 90% of volcanic origin and divides into a hot coastal belt, subtropical central valleys and plateaux and northern mountains. El Salvador is the most densely populated country in America; the population is 60% rural and concentrated largely in the central area. The economy is mainly agricultural. Half the work-force is engaged in growing coffee, cotton, maize, sugar and sorghum and grazing animals. Coffee is the main crop and makes up 51% of exports; El Salvador is very vulnerable to a drop in world coffee prices and past falls have pushed the country into the arms of the IMF. Industry has developed considerably during the 1970s. A high standard of cotton textiles is produced along with food, drink, footwear and oil and chemical products. The country is the leading exporter of manufactured goods in Central America. In 1980 a new pharmaceutical plant was established and a silver mine re-opened. In addition to coffee, sugar, cotton and shrimp are exported. Over a quarter of exports go to the USA and the rest to Central America, the EEC and Japan. Food, consumer goods and capital goods are imported, notably wheat and flour, oil, fertilizer, machinery and vehicles. Sources are the same as export partners. Primary and secondary education are free and compulsory. Between 1967 and 1972 the government built new schools at the rate of one a day. There is a national university and a Roman Catholic university. There are 10 900 km of roads, half of which can only be used in the dry season. There is a social security system. Recent civil strife must be damaging the economy but figures are not available.

Ethiopia

Population:	31.1m.
GNP:	$3bn.
Growth rate per capita:	0.5%
Development assistance per capita:	$4.66
Literacy rate:	7%
International affiliations:	UN, OAU, ICO, ACP, Group of 77, N/A
Defence expenditure:	$385m.

Ethiopia, the oldest independent country in Africa (fifth century BC), is situated in the Horn of Africa with Sudan to the west, Kenya to the south, the Somali Republic and Djibouti to the east and a north-western coastline along the Red Sea. The Great Rift Valley runs diagonally across the high central plateau of the country. The main activity which employs 86% of the work-force is traditional agriculture with low productivity. There is a serious problem of soil erosion and deforestation. Coffee is the major crop, producing 50% of exports. Cereals, pulses and oilseeds are also grown. 53% of the land is pastoral and in 1978, 27.5 million cattle, 23.2 million sheep and 17.1 million goats were grazing on it. Hides, skins and meat are also exported. Ethiopia is nearly self-sufficient in agriculture but since 1972 severe drought has caused many deaths and reduced herds. Fighting in Eritrea and the Ogaden has further damaged agricultural production. A small amount of industry, principally in processing food and textiles, has grown up around Addis Ababa, the capital in the centre of the country. Industry around Asmara in Eritrea in the north has been damaged in hostilities. Copper mining in the same area declined for the same reason. Gold and a little platinum are mined and potash reserves await exploitation. Ethiopia imports manufactured goods, transport equipment, oil, food and textiles. Main trading partners are the USA, West Germany, Italy and Japan. Development depends on foreign aid which accounts for more than a third of the budget. In 1975 there were 872 000 school-children but higher education was closed and the students sent to the countryside as political teachers in the *cemetcha* campaign. There are 8 000 km of all-weather roads and about half the population lives within a day's walk of such a road. Railway services are limited and were suspended during fighting.

Fiji

Population:	0.62m.
GNP:	$710m.
Growth rate per capita:	3.4%
Development assistance per capita:	$37.24
Literacy rate:	85%
International affiliations:	UN, CW, AOB, Colombo Plan; Pacific regional bodies
Defence expenditure:	$3.62m.

Fiji lies in the centre of the South Pacific islands, about 2 080 km north of New Zealand. The 180th meridian passes through the group but the international dateline is set further east. Fiji consists of 800 islands and islets, of which 105 are inhabited. The main island is Vita Levu and like the others is mountainous and volcanic in origin. Europeans introduced rum, guns, disease and chaos and subsequently sugar and banana plantations and Indian labour. The later innovations continue although banana production has been severely affected by disease and hurricanes. 83% of the land belongs to village groups – 'mataqalis' and is administered by the Native Land Trust Board. 50% of the population are Indian, who are allowed to lease land for 10 years. Copra and ginger are also grown. Cattle raising and the rearing of horses, goats and pigs are developing fast. There is a comprehensive scheme of pine planting. Tuna is fished and canned. Sugar is the vital crop, grown by 17 000 independent farmers and marketed by a state corporation. It accounts for two-thirds of exports, one fifth of GDP and employs a quarter of all wage-earners. Copra is the other main export. As an island economy, Fiji needs to import food, machinery, manufactured goods, fuel and chemicals and has an increasing trade deficit, partially offset by expanding tourism. Australia, Japan, UK, New Zealand and Canada are the main partners. Education is not compulsory and about half is free but attendance is virtually 100% of the school-age group. Students attend the University of the South Pacific which uses a NASA satellite for educational exchange with universities in Hawaii and Alaska. There has been heavy spending on roads; there is 640 km of railway for sugar; Nadi, the international airport, is a staging post between the USA and Australia. The Fiji School of Medicine founded in 1885 is a Pacific regional centre.

Gabon

Population:	0.584m.
GNP	$3bn.
Growth rate per capita:	6.1%
Development assistance per capita:	$62.08
Literacy rate:	30%
International affiliations:	UN, OAU, OCAM, UDEAC, ACP, OPEC, Group of 77, N/A
Defence expenditure:	(2 800 troops)

Gabon, a former French colony, lies on the Equator on the west coast of Africa with the Congo to the south and east, Equatorial Guinea and Cameroon to the north. The country is 75% tropical rainforest which drains into the Ogoove River, at the mouth of which is the industrial centre of Port-Gentil. The capital, on the mouth of the Como River, is called Libreville as it was founded by freed slaves in 1849. The population density is extremely low and there is a great labour shortage. The population is also diverse, consisting of 40 different ethnic groups intermingled. 70% of the work-force grows a small amount of coffee and cocoa and raises cattle and sheep but less than one per cent of land is cultivated and 90% of food has to be imported. Nevertheless, Gabon has a high per capita GDP for Africa and a trade surplus, all because of oil which accounted for 85% of exports in 1977. Oil revenues have financed rapid development of oil, mineral and wood-processing industry. The country mines iron ore and uranium but above all manganese, of which no country exports more. Oil replaced wood as the main export in 1963 and with the proceeds, not only food but construction equipment, machinery, vehicles and manufactured goods are also imported. Education from 6–16 is compulsory and there is a national university at Libreville. The 1975 Infrastructure Development Plan projected work on roads, sea and airports. The Trans-Gabon railway, designed to open up the interior was due for completion in 1979.

The fact that 46% of the population is Christian has led some to describe Gabon as 'the bastion of the cross in Africa'.

The Gambia

Population:	0.493m.
GNP:	$230m.
Growth rate per capita:	4.8%
Development assistance per capita	$24.07
Literacy rate:	10%
International affiliations:	UN, CW, OAU, ACP, Group of 77, N/A
Defence expenditure:	n/a

The Gambia, a former British colony, is an enclave in Senegal on the west coast of West Africa. It consists of a 320 km strip of land, 11 to 32 km wide along the banks of the Gambia River. The terrain near the river is low-lying and covered in thick mangrove swamps; away from the river there are sand-hills and plateaux. The climate is subtropical with rain concentrated in the summer and temperatures rising to 110°F. The economy is almost entirely based on agriculture which involves the growing of insufficient subsistence crops of rice, millet and sorghum and the main export crop of groundnuts, on 55% of the land by 85% of the work-force. There is some livestock and fishing increased in the 1970s. Most cultivable land is planted with groundnuts, industry centres around groundnut processing, and groundnuts and groundnut oil account for 95% of exports. The government wants to diversify. The UK and the rest of the EEC import the groundnuts and supply in return textiles, food, machinery and transport equipment. Tourism is growing. Palm kernels, fish, hides and skins are also exported. In 1976 there were 24 800 school-children. Transport is essentially on the river, navigable by ocean vessels up to 150 miles and 138 miles farther by smaller craft. There is no army.

Ghana

Population:	11.4m.
GNP:	$10.8bn.
Growth rate per capita:	−2.1%

Development assistance
per capita: $9.27
Literacy rate: 25%
International affiliations: UN, CW, OAU, ECOWAS,
                               ACP(EEC)
Defence expenditure: $155m.

Ghana lies a few degrees north of the Equator in the middle
of the south coast of West Africa on the Gulf of Guinea. The
coastal region of scrubland and plains is dry in the east and
humid in the west near the frontier with Togo. In the south-
western region bordering on the Ivory Coast and the central
Ashanti region there is tropical rainforest. The north of the
country is dry savana and bush spreading up to the frontier
with Upper Volta. Ghana grows a variety of cash crops
including coconuts, coffee and tobacco but cocoa beans and
their products form two-thirds of exports. Maize, plantains,
rice, cassava and groundnuts are grown for local consumption
and the country is self-sufficient in livestock and poultry.
Sugar-cane, oilpalm, kenaf and rubber are harvested to supply local industry to meet local requirements. Agriculture
occupies 60% of the work-force and 70% of the land. As well
as processing agricultural products, Ghanaian industry
produces textiles, steel from scrap metal, refined oil products,
assembled vehicles and aluminium from imported alumina.
Most industrial activity is by way of import substitution but
aluminium is exported. Gold and manganese ore are exported
and natural resources also include bauxite, iron ore and
diamonds. Offshore oil was discovered in 1978. Imports are
oil, food, industrial raw materials, machinery and transport
equipment. The USA and the UK are the main partners.
Ghana's development since independence has been unsteady.
Over-ambitious public investment drained reserves and forced repudiation of debt schedules and restrictions of imports. From 1976 to 1978, inflation and unemployment were
high and real per capita income declined. Food shortages
caused demonstrations and strikes in 1977. The government
launched crash programmes: 'Operation Feed Yourself' and
'Operation Feed Your Industries'; the cultivated area was
expanded. From ages 6–15 education is free; primary education is compulsory; there are three universities.

Guatemala

Population:	6.95m.
GNP:	$6.6bn.
Growth rate per capita:	3.3%
Development assistance per capita:	$9.01
Literacy rate:	38%
International affiliations:	UN, OAS, CACM
Defence expenditure:	$76.8m.

Guatemala is the most populous and northernmost of the Central American republics, independent as a separate nation since 1840. Inland from the southern coast on the Pacific are the highlands and mountains whose southern slopes are well-watered and fertile. The bulk of the population and the capital, Guatemala City, are in this region. To the north of the mountains is a sparsely populated third of the country and to the north-east, a short Caribbean coastline, between Belize and Honduras, subject to high rainfall, devastating to crops. Mexico lies to the north and west and El Salvador and Honduras to the east. Agriculture occupies 25% of the land and 60% of the work-force and produces 30% of the GDP. Coffee, cotton and bananas are grown for export and corn and beans for consumption. Production of these crops rose during the 1970s but Guatemala still has to import grain, so the state requires farmers to grow minimum amounts of grain. $2\frac{1}{2}$ million cattle provide meat exports. Forests are unevenly exploited, some too much, others too little. The main forest crop is chicle gum (second largest output in the world) used in chewing gum. Industry is small but led economic growth in the sixties and early seventies and employs 11% of the work-force producing 16% of GDP. Main activities are construction, textiles, food-processing, tyres and pharmaceuticals. Industrial exports go to the rest of Central America and agricultural products go also to the USA, Germany and Japan. Manufactured goods, machinery, transport equipment, chemicals, fuels and food are imported from these same three. Current priorities are to help the rural poor but development is hampered by inflation, high oil prices and a rapid increase in population. Agrarian reform has muddled along since 1952. There has been 'comprehensive social security' since 1946. The population is half Amerindian and half *mestizo* (mixed).

Guinea

Population:	5.35m.
GNP:	$740m.
Growth rate per capita:	1.7%
Development assistance per capita:	$3
Literacy rate:	10%
International affiliations:	UN, OAU, ACP(EEC)
Defence expenditure:	(9 200 troops)

Guinea is on the south-west coast of West Africa. Most of the country has two rainy seasons a year and is very hot and humid (74–85°F, 422 cm). 84% of workers are engaged in agriculture producing rice, cassava, millet and maize for local consumption and pineapples, bananas, palm kernels and coffee for export. The Foutah Djallon region is devoted to cattle raising. The chief source of income are mineral reserves. Guinea is believed to have one-third of the world's reserves of bauxite. The principal industry is the production of bauxite and alumina, which together amount to 88% of exports. The industry is a joint venture involving large amounts of foreign capital. There are also plans to extract 15 million tons of iron ore per annum from a mine at Nimba. Diamonds and gold are also found. There is some light manufacturing. Main imports are: oil, raw materials, machinery, transport equipment and food. Main partners are Western European countries, the USA, and communist countries. About 17% of school-age children are in full-time education. There is a highway running though southern Guinea into Liberia to the port of Monrovia. The constitution provides for the limitation of sovereignty in favour of African unity.

Guinea-Bissau

Population:	0.640m.
GNP:	$174m.
Growth rate per capita:	n/a
Development assistance per capita:	$43.21
Literacy rate:	5%
International affiliations:	UN, OAU, CEAO, ACP, Group of 77, N/A
Defence expenditure:	(6 100 troops)

A former colony of Portuguese Guinea on the south-west face of West Africa's bulge, Guinea-Bissau has Senegal to the north, Guinea to the south and east. The land is swamp on the coast and irrigated by the rivers Cacheu, Geba and Corubal rising to savanna inland. The hinterland is hardwood forest, then grassland and trees. Average temperature: 77°F; rain: 175cm. The wet season is June to November. The rest of the year is dry and the *harmathan*, the dust-laden wind from the Sahara, blows.

From 1959 to 1974 there was armed struggle between the PAIGC, the independence party and the Portuguese, which left the economy in need of complete re-building. The economic base remains agriculture and cattle. There were plans for self-sufficiency in rice by 1979.

Crops: Groundnuts, rice, palm oil, coconuts
Animals: 262 000 cattle reared specially for their hides, pigs, goats
Industry: Palm oil, hides and skins, beer, soft drinks
Minerals: Bauxite, oil exploration in progress
Exports: Palm oil, groundnuts, timber, coconuts, hides, skins
Imports: Manufactured goods, fuels, rice, food products
Trading partners: Portugal, Spain, UK, Japan, Italy, Cape Verde Islands.

Guyana

Population:	0.830m.
GNP:	$470m.
Growth rate per capita:	− 0.3%
Development assistance per capita:	$14.74
Literacy rate:	86%
International affiliations:	UN, CW, GATT, OAS, ACP, Group of 77, N/A
Defence expenditure:	$17m.

Former British colony, independent 1970, on the north-east coast of South America; Venezuela to the west, Brazil to the south, Surinam to the east. Agriculture is concentrated on the coastal plain. 85% of the country is forest. There is some savanna. Guyana is developing a co-operative-based socialist economy, exporting processed agricultural products as well as raw materials and importing capital and consumer goods. Income is relatively evenly distributed. Unemployment: 15%. Voluntary national service (necessary for a place at university) involves work camps, clearing land and planting crops. There are bans on certain imports to encourage the development of indigenous alternatives. The government has invested in roads, irrigation and electric power, notably the Upper Mazaruni Hydro-electric Project.

Private education was abolished in 1976. The government provides education from nursery to university. Railway: 130 km; roads: 2 320 km. No road or rail links with neighbours but link to Pan-American highway under construction. Venezuela claims five-eighths of Guyana's territory.

Crops: Sugar, rice
Agricultural land: 15% of total, much unused; labour 30%
Minerals: Alumina, bauxite
Exports: Sugar, bauxite and alumina, rice, shrimp, rum, timber, molasses
Imports: Wheat and flour, milk, textiles, footwear, motor vehicles and parts
Trading partners: Canada, Caricom, EEC, China, UK, USSR, USA, Japan

Haiti

Population:	5.7m.
GNP:	$1.3bn.
Growth rate per capita:	2.5%
Development assistance per capita:	$15.67
Literacy rate:	30%
International affiliations:	UN, OAS, GATT, IMF, IBRD
Defence expenditure:	$18.4m

Former French colony, independent since 1804 slave revolt, occupying western third of the Caribbean island of Hispaniola, between Puerto Rico and Cuba. Two-thirds of the land is mountainous and uncultivable. The climate is dry, tropical except for the humid coast; average temperature: 70–90°F. Development is hampered by low agricultural productivity, disease and lack of educated and skilled labour. There is a shortage of foreign exchange.

Primary education is free; in 1974 only 14% of rural children attended school. There is a 160 km-long railway for sugar only.

Agriculture: labour 83%, land (potential) 33%, divided into over half-million small family plots
Crops: Coffee, sugar, sisal, tropical fruits, cocoa, rice, maize, tubers, tobacco
Animals: Cattle, horses, pigs
Industry: Light manufacturing, ore processing, handicrafts, labour-intensive assembly of consumer goods for export (centred around Port-au-Prince, the capital)
Minerals: Bauxite, copper
Exports: Coffee, sugar, bauxite, essential oils, handicrafts, light manufactures. Partners: USA (50%), Belgium
Imports: Machinery, food, oil, textiles. Partners: USA (70%), Japan, France

Hong Kong

Population:	4.5m.
GNP	$2 381
Growth rate per capita:	6.2%
Development assistance per capita:	$0.39
Literacy rate:	75%
International affiliations:	(British Crown Colony)

Hong Kong consists of more than 200 islands, of which Hong Kong Island and Lan Tao are the only large ones, and the Kowloon Peninsula, adjacent to the province of Kwantung on China's south-eastern coast. Around the colony's natural harbour are the two cities of Victoria and Kowloon. Hong Kong is mainly hilly but the new territories, leased to Britain until 1997, are flat and cultivated. The economic basis of Hong Kong is trade, supplemented by light manufacturing industry. Water is scarce in winter. Official policy is laissez-faire; taxes are low; nearly all annual budgets have been surplus since the second world war.

Crops: Some vegetables; most food is imported from China.
Animals: Pigs, chicken, cattle
Land: 78% of Hong Kong is uncultivable, 8% urban, 14% arable
Industry: Textiles and clothing, toys, transistor radios,

watches, electrical parts; light industry generally in multi-purpose built factories. Heavy industry developing: ship-building, aircraft, engineering, iron and steel
Exports: Clothing and textiles, toys, plastic flowers, watches, radios
Imports: Raw materials, semi-manufactured goods, consumer goods
Main Partners: USA, Japan, China, UK, West Germany, Taiwan, Singapore
Education: Primary, free and compulsory. Secondary, free (and compulsion being introduced); two universities
Communications: Modern airport and port (focus for contact with China); modernized railway to Canton and underground railway

India

Population:	673m.
GNP:	$96bn.
Growth rate per capita:	1.4%
Development assistance per capita:	$2.16
Literacy rate:	34%
International affiliations:	UN, CW, Colombo Plan, ADB, IMF, IAEA, IBRD, N/A
Defence expenditure:	$4.4bn.

Indian civilization goes back two and a half millennia, but modern India gained its independence in 1947 when the British Raj was partitioned into India and Pakistan. There is a long coastline on the Arabian Sea, the Indian Ocean and the Bay of Bengal; the north-eastern part of the country borders on Nepal and Bangladesh. India is the second most populous country (after China) and at least 42% of the population is under 15. The death-rate has dropped considerably with the eradication of plague (1967) and smallpox (1975), economic progress since independence and an increase in medical staff (doctors × 2½, nurses × 5 in last 25 years). Despite a strong industrial base and skilled labour, unemployment is rising. Development plans have concentrated on family planning, agriculture, mining and manufacturing; the 6th Plan (1978–83) stresses energy, science and technology, industry and communications. A major objective is to reduce rural poverty; cottage industry is encouraged and capital-intensive alternatives restricted. *Parchayati Raj* (village democracy) has been revived in most parts and the official ideology is socialism.

Natural resources: Iron ore, mica, bauxite, limestone, coal
Crops: Rice, wheat, pulses, oilseeds, cotton, tea (N.B. 70% of world's cardamon production)
Animals: Cattle, sheep, pigs. An intensive cattle development project is under way.
Agriculture: 74% population, 54% land, 40% GNP
Industry: Textiles, cotton and jute, processed food, steel, machinery, cement; a growing motor industry; oil refining (meeting 65% home demand). Also 20 million people in traditional village industries: weaving, silk, shawls, carpets, wood and metal work
Energy: 93 hydro-electric and 5 nuclear power stations
Exports: Engineering goods, cotton textiles, handicrafts, tea, iron, steel
Imports: Oil, foodgrains, machinery, fertilizer
Partners: USA, Japan, UK, USSR, West Germany
Education: 9 years compulsory (unenforceable) with incentives; attendance 83% (6–11), 38% (11–14), 21% (14–17); 108 universities
Communications: 1.3 million km of road; 60 000 km of rail; 14 150 km of navigable waterway

Indonesia

Population:	149.6m.
GNP:	$43.1bn.
Growth rate per capita:	5.5%
Development assistance per capita:	$4.40
Literacy rate:	n/a
International affiliations:	UN, ASEAN, Colombo Plan
Defence expenditure:	$2.07m.

Indonesia, a former Dutch colony independent since 1950, consists of several groups of islands, 13 500 in all, spreading for 4 800 km along the Equator between Asia and Australia and between the Indian and Pacific Oceans. The islands include Sumatra, Java, Bali and Sulawesi; also the southern part of Borneo (Kalimantan) bordering on Malaysia and the western part of New Guinea (Irian Jaya) bordering on Papua New Guinea. The climate is tropical, the terrain mountainous and volcanic in general. Given the natural resources available, development has been disappointing. In the post-independence period the infrastructure and GNP declined, foreign debts and inflation mounted and foreign investment was low. Debts have been re-scheduled and following an IMF-backed stabilization period foreign investment (from the Philippines, South Korea, Malaysia, Hong Kong and the USA) has increased and inflation dropped. Development priorities have been to improve living standards for the 30 million rural poor. Java, Bali, and Madura are overpopulated and rice production grows more slowly than population, so food has to be imported.

Natural Resources: Oil, timber, nickel, natural gas, tin, bauxite, copper
Crops: Rice, cassava, soybeans, copra, rubber, coffee, tea, palm oil
Forestry: 60% of the land has been described as a 'green gold mine' but exploitation is low, most paper is still imported.
Agriculture: 11% of the land, 61% of the workforce
Industry: Textiles, food and beverages, manufactures, cement, fertilizer, 8 oil refineries, shipyards, construction
Energy: 3 large hydro-electric plants; nuclear reactors
Exports: Oil, timber, rubber, tin, coffee, palm-oil, tea, tobacco, copra
Imports: Food, chemicals, textiles, oil, rice, consumer goods, fertilizer, iron, steel, machinery
Partners: Japan, USA, Malaysia and Singapore, West Germany
Education: In theory free and compulsory from 6–12; in practice 80% primary attendance, 15% secondary, 51 universities
Communications: PELNI, the national shipping company, is central. A trans-Sumatra trunk road is planned.

Iran

Population:	38.23m.
GNP:	$76.1bn.
Growth rate per capita:	n/a
Development assistance per capita:	$0.11
Literacy rate:	36%

International affiliations:	UN, OPEC, IAEA, IMF, IBRD
Defence expenditure:	$4.2bn.

Iran lies between the Persian Gulf and the Caspian Sea with Iraq and Turkey on its eastern frontiers, the USSR to the north and Afghanistan and Pakistan to the East. The capital Tehran, in the north, has a population of four and a half million; the second largest city, Isfahan, has a population of 575 000 and is a textile centre. Traditionally an agricultural country, modern Iran's rapid but uneven development has relied upon oil which was nationalized in 1951. In general, 70% of oil revenues has been devoted to economic and social development. The interior is a mixture of deserts and highlands surrounded by mountains. Rain varies from 20 to 100 cm.

The population is only 63% Persian, the rest being Kurd, Turkoman, Baluchi, Arab and other minorities.

Natural resources: Oil, gas, iron, copper
Crops: Wheat, barley, oats, rice, sugar, tobacco, beets, cotton, dates, tea
Agricultural land: 14%, a third of which needs irrigation by ditches, wells and tunnels
Labour force: 37% agriculture, 27% industry
Industry: Oil, petrochemicals, textiles, cement, food-processing, steel, aluminium, metal, fabrics, assembly of motor vehicles
Exports: Petroleum 87%, carpets, cotton, fruits, nuts, hides, leather, ores
Imports: Machinery, iron and steel, chemicals, pharmaceuticals, electrical
Partners: USA, Germany, Japan, USSR
Education: Primary and secondary available to 80% of children; three universities in Tehran, and five elsewhere
Health: There have been successful campaigns against malaria and opium addiction.
Communications: 10 000 km of surfaced road; 5 000 km of railway

Iraq

Population:	13.11m.
GNP:	$21.4bn.
Growth rate per capita:	6.9%

Development assistance	
per capita:	$3.49
Literacy rate:	51%
International affiliations:	UN, Arab League, OAPEC, associate member of Comecon
Defence expenditure:	$2.67bn.

Iraq has a small coastline on the Persian Gulf but is otherwise landlocked with Kuwait and Saudi Arabia to the south, Iran to the east, Turkey to the north and Syria and Jordan to the west. To the south and west the land is mainly desert; in the north are mountains; the fertile plain of Mesopotamia between the Tigris and the Euphrates runs from the north-west to marshes in the south-east. The capital Baghdad (pop. 3.5 million) lies in that plain. Iraq is hot and dry, up to 120°F in summer and below freezing sometimes in January. 10–17 cm of rain.

Natural resources: Oil, natural gas, phosphates, sulphur
Crops: Wheat, barley and vegetables (winter) cotton, fruits, dates and vegetables (summer)
Animals: Large farms for cattle and poultry have been constructed; also buffaloes, sheep and goats
Industry: Petroleum, cement, textiles, construction, bricks, water and electricity. Iron and steel and petrochemicals are being developed.
Exports: Petroleum, dates
Imports: Manufactured goods, foodgrains, machinery, construction material
Main partners: Western Europe, Japan, USSR, USA
Education: Compulsory 6–12, free 6–15; 45% attendance, 5 universities
Communications: 9 600 km of road and track

Ivory Coast

Population:	8.2m.
GNP:	$7.7bn.
Growth rate per capita:	1.3%
Development assistance	
per capita:	$21.16
Literacy rate:	20%
International affiliations:	UN, OAU, CEAO, OCAM, ACP, IAEA
Defence expenditure:	$89.2m.

The Ivory Coast, a former French colony independent since 1960, lies on the south coast of West Africa, east of Liberia and west of Ghana. To the north-west is Guinea; Mali and Upper Volta are to the north. The country is flat with coastal lagoons in the south-east where the commercial centre and capital, Abidjan, is found. Abidjan has been called the Brussels of West Africa because of its commercial and political role. Inland there is tropical forest where the cash crops are grown and further north there is sandy savanna. Development has been rapid since 1950. The 4th Development Plan (1976–80) pursued the traditional aim of agricultural diversity and expansion together with a high level of public spending on infrastructure and export industry. The government's policy is to encourage private enterprise, increasingly in indigenous hands. The population is very diverse consisting of over 60 ethnic groups with a correspondingly large number of dialects. French is the official language.

Natural resources: Offshore petroleum, unexploited iron ore, diamonds, manganese
Crops: Coffee, cocoa, palm oil, sugar, bananas
Animals: Cattle, sheep, goats, pigs
Agriculture: 75% work-force, 25% GDP, production doubled 1968–78
Industry: Construction, food, textiles, shoes, metal; 25% work-force, 15% GDP; production × 11, 1960–77
Exports: Coffee, tropical woods (including mahogany), cocoa
Imports: Semi-finished products, raw materials, consumer goods, cement, fuel
Partners: EEC (especially France) and USA
Education: 12 years compulsory, 62% attendance; University of Abidjan
Communications: There is a railway to Upper Volta.

Jamaica

Population:	2.25m.
GNP:	$3.17bn.
Growth rate per capita:	− 1.5%
Development assistance per capita:	$14.17
Literacy rate:	65%
International affiliations:	UN, OAS, ACP, CW, GATT, IBRD, Caricom
Defence expenditure:	$17m.

Jamaica, a former British colony independent since 1962, is the third-largest island in the Caribbean, lying south of Cuba and west of Haiti. 80% of the island is mountainous. The climate is tropical and humid with rainfall varying from 500 cm to nothing in different parts. The capital, Kingston (population 600 000), is on the south coast. The traditional economic base was formed by plantation sugar cane and bananas. There are severe economic problems including high unemployment, a high birth rate, a high level of emigration and balance of payments deficits. The return of Edward Seaga's Jamaican Labour Party in 1981 suggests that the emphasis will now swing to private enterprise and attracting foreign investment.

Natural resources: Bauxite and alumina, gypsum, limestone
Crops: Sugar, bananas, citrus, coffee, pimento, allspice
Animals: Cattle, goats, pigs, poultry
Agriculture: 42% of land, 29% of work-force
Industry: Bauxite, textiles, food-processing, sugar, rum, molasses, cement, metal, paper, tyres, chemicals; oil refining (Kingston); also tourism
Exports: Alumina, bauxite, sugar, bananas
Imports: Machinery, transport equipment, electrical, food, fuel, fertilizer
Partners: USA, UK, Caricom, Venezuela, Norway, Canada, Japan
Education: Free and compulsory until 14; primary attendance – 75%, secondary – 25%
Communications: 4 800 km of main roads; 7 000 secondary; 337 km of railway, 19 ports, two international airports

Jordan

Population:	3.14m.
GNP:	$2.69bn.
Growth rate per capita:	8.8%
Development assistance per capita:	$48.53
Literacy rate:	55%
International affiliations:	Arab League, UN, IAEA, IBRD, IMF
Defence expenditure:	$381m.

Jordan, a former British mandated territory independent since 1946, lies in the heart of the Middle East with a very short coastline on the Gulf of Aqaba at the head of the Red Sea, Saudi Arabia to the south and east, Iraq to the north-east, Syria to the north and Israel along the western frontier. The west bank of the river Jordan is occupied by Israel. Despite few natural resources and a paucity of cultivable land, Jordan developed rapidly in the 1960s. Economic problems of high unemployment, inflation, a limited domestic market and the emigration of skilled labour are aggravated by the presence of over a million Palestinian refugees, the loss of the West Bank and the continued political uncertainty in the Middle East. 88% of Jordan is desert or waste. The Jordan rift valley runs north through Lake Tiberias (Galilee) and the Dead Sea.

Natural resources: Phosphate, potash (Dead Sea)
Crops: Wheat, fruit, vegetables, olive oil
Animals: Sheep, goats, cattle, camels
Agriculture: 11% of land (increasing through terracing and irrigation); 23% of work-force
Industry: Phosphate, petroleum-refining, cement; 67% of work-force
Exports: Fruit, vegetables, phosphates, light manufactures
Imports: Machinery, transport equipment, cereals, petroleum products, manufactures, food, drink, tobacco
Partners: Saudi Arabia, EEC, USA, Syria, Iraq, Kuwait, Lebanon
Education : About 600 000 school-children; University of Jordan

Kampuchea

Population:	8.6m.
GNP per capita:	$102
Growth rate per capita:	n/a
Development assistance per capita:	$3.32
Literacy rate:	n/a
International affiliations:	(The UN and other organizations recognize the exiled Pol Pot régime)
Defence expenditure:	n/a

Kampuchea, formerly Cambodia, a French protectorate independent since 1953, is in South East Asia with an irregular coastline on the west of the Gulf of Siam; Thailand to the west and north, Laos to the north-east and Vietnam to the east and south. The Mekong river runs through the centre of the country and provides excellent rice-growing conditions. The climate is tropical monsoon, dry from October to May; rain – 145 cm. Between 1975 and 1979, the cities were emptied and the population driven into collectivized agriculture; irrigation was developed and double-and treble-cropping introduced, resulting in rice exports in 1976. Floods in 1978 and fighting in 1979 ruined crops and restricted new planting. In 1980 there was widespread famine which eventually forced the new Heng Samrin government to accept international aid. There were no currency, civil servants, technicians, doctors or teachers. The process of re-construction continues with re-planting and the development of safe water supplies.

Natural resources: Timber, gemstones, iron ore, manganese, phosphate
Crops: Rice, rubber
Forestry: 20 million acres of largely unexploited forest
Industry: (Pre-1970): textiles, cement, rubber products, motor vehicle assembly. Power and water have been restored to Phnom Penh, the capital, and some small factories are open.
Exports: Dried fish, rubber; (potential export: rice)
Imports: Rice, petroleum, lubricants, machinery, insecticide
Partners: Thailand, China, Pakistan (virtually no trade 1979–80)
Education: In July 1979, 50 000 were said to be at school.
Health: Malaria has been a major problem, combated by DDT.

Kenya

Population:	15.8m.
GNP:	$6.3bn.
Growth rate per capita:	1.2%
Development assistance per capita:	$10.95
Literacy rate:	15–20%
International affiliations:	UN, OAU, CW, ACP, Group of 77, N/A
Defence expenditure:	$168m.

Kenya, a former British colony independent since 1963, lies across the Equator in East Africa, with the Somali Republic and the Indian Ocean to the east, Tanzania to the south, Uganda to the west, the Sudan to the north-west and Ethiopia to the north. In the northern part of the country the life-style is nomadic and pastoral. There is a tropical coastal region in the south, including the main port of Mombasa. Moving inland, there is scrub, then the Great Rift Valley and then mountains and plateaux sloping down to Lake Victoria. Temperatures vary from 80°F on the coast to 67°F in Nairobi, the capital. The economic life of the country and 85% of the population lives in the south. The republic has adopted the motto *Harambee* meaning 'pull together' and volunteer programmes exist for building schools and clinics. There is a strong policy of Africanization coupled with the maintenance of a mixed economy and the encouragement of foreign investment.

Natural resources: Soda ash, limestone, gold (exploration with UN help in the west)
Crops: Coffee, tea, pyrethrum, maize, wheat, rice, sisal, sugarcane
Forestry: Coniferous, hardwoods and bamboo; growing exports
Agriculture: 10–15% land for crops; 80% for livestock and game; 75% of work-force
Industry: Petroleum products, cement, beer; light consumer goods; agricultural products (centred on Nairobi, with oil-refining and ship-repairing at Mombasa); 14% of work-force; 11% of GDP
Exports: Coffee, petroleum products, tea, hides and skins, meat, cement, pyrethrum
Imports: Crude petroleum, machinery, vehicles, iron and steel, paper, pharmaceuticals, fertilizer
Partners: EEC (especially UK), USA, Canada, Zambia, Japan, Australia
Education: None compulsory; four years primary free; secondary built and run on self-help basis; 4 000 students at University of Nairobi

Korea,   Democratic People's Republic of (North)
Population: 17.58m.
GNP: $10.5bn.
Growth rate per capita: n/a

Development assistance
per capita: n/a
Literacy rate: 90%
International affiliations: UN observer, Comecon
                          observer, Colombo Plan
Defence expenditure: $1.3bn.

Korea was originally divided at the Yalta Conference; the two
parts went to war in 1950 but recently a dialogue has
developed. The Korean peninsula juts out from north-east
China with the Yellow Sea to the west and the Sea of Japan to
the east. There is a short land frontier with the USSR in the
north-east. Industrial development started in the 1920s and
1930s while Korea was annexed to Japan. After the division the
north contained most of the natural resources and two-thirds
of heavy industry. The economy is centrally controlled and has
developed rapidly. During the 1971–76 6-year-plan engineering industry multiplied by a factor of 2.4. The 1978–84 7-year-
plan gives priority to fuel, mining, foreign trade and transport.
The People's Assembly elected in 1979 announced a national
drive to increase poultry, fish and edible oil production.

Natural resources: Coal, iron ore, graphite, tungsten, zinc,
lead, copper, manganese, cobalt, phosphates, gold, silver
Crops: Maize, rice, vegetables (highly mechanized with
modern irrigation)
Forestry: Afforestation programme includes oil-bearing trees.
Agriculture: 50% of work-force, 17% of land (state or co-
operative owned)
Industry: Machines, chemicals and fertilizers, minerals and
metals, textiles
Energy: Thermal and hydro-electric plants; oil pipeline from
China, oilwells; coal mines
Exports: Metal ores and products
Imports: Machinery and petroleum products
Partners: 86% Communist countries (53% USSR); large
foreign debts (esp. Japan)
Education: 11 years free and compulsory, two-thirds of
students at the 150 higher education establishments study
technology or engineering; three main universities
Health: Medical treatment is free.
Communications: One third of the country without railways;
roads are bad. Railways built by Japan; 66% of trains were
electrified by 1979. Ports have been developed and expanded.

Korea,   Republic of (South)

Population:	38.2m.
GNP:	$46bn.
Growth rate per capita:	8.0%
Development assistance per capita:	$6.33
Literacy rate:	90%
International affiliation:	UN observer, ADB, Colombo Plan, IAEA, IBRD
Defence expenditure:	$3.46bn.

South Korea has a land frontier (de-militarized zone) with North Korea and a sea-frontier with Japan across the Korea–Kaikyo straits. (See North Korea for geography). The country is densely populated and low in natural resources. However, rapid industrialization and substantial foreign investments coupled with low wages have produced high growth rates led by exports of manufactured goods. There have been problems with the balance of payments and inflation, notably after increases in oil prices. 28% of the budget is for defence. Development plans conceived 1980 as the deadline for self-sufficiency, especially in rice. The capital, Seoul, lies within 48 km of North Korea and has more than 6½ million inhabitants.

Crops: Rice, barley, wheat, tobacco (state monopoly); self-sufficient in grain since 1976
Animals: Cattle, hogs, poultry
Fishing: Deep-sea and inshore; Indian and Pacific Oceans
Agriculture: 23% of land, 25% of GNP
Industry: Textiles, clothing, food-processing, chemicals, fertilizers, plywood, coal, electronics, steel; recent shift toward heavy and petro-chemical industries
Exports: Clothing, plywood, electrical products, iron and steel, wigs, footwear, silk
Imports: Petroleum products, machinery, wood, chemicals, cotton, ore, metal scrap, vehicles
Partners: Japan, USA
Education: Primary – compulsory, attendance 98%; 215 universities and colleges; over 9 million in full-time education
Communications: Most of country connected to Seoul by motorway; railways extensive

Kuwait

Population:	1.31m.
GNP:	$11.9bn.
Growth rate per capita:	−0.9%
Development assistance per capita:	$1.84
Literacy rate:	80%
International affiliations:	Arab League, UN, OPEC, OAPEC, IMF, World Bank, IBRD, Group of 77, N/A
Defence expenditure:	$979m.

Kuwait lies at the head of the Persian Gulf between Iraq and Saudi Arabia. In 1961 Britain handed back responsibility for foreign affairs. Historically, the country was an entrepot for the interior but this role has declined. Oil, first exploited in 1937 and now mainly owned by the government, has transformed the country. Oil revenues are spent on social welfare, development and public works: schools, roads and hospitals. The majority of the population is not indigenous and has been sucked in by economic growth, from surrounding countries. The capital, Kuwait, is the major port and commercial centre with a population of 800 000. Kuwait gives aid to developing countries, mainly Arab ones.

Crops: Melons, tomatoes, onion, radishes, clover; most food imported; experiments in hydroponics
Animals: Cattle, sheep, goats, poultry
Fishing: Inshore and ocean (Indian and Atlantic) on a large scale; shrimp
Agriculture: Arable land less than 1%
Industry: Natural gas, petroleum-refining, commerce, public-sector-government and services; fertilizer, chemicals, water de-salinization (largest distillation plant in world), boat-building
Exports: 96% crude and refined petroleum
Imports: Food, animals, vehicles, construction materials, machinery, textiles
Partners: EEC, USA, Japan
Education and Health: Free; Government pays for students to study abroad as well; 6 500 students at Kuwait university

Laos

Population:	3.4m.
GNP:	$260m.
Growth rate per capita:	n/a
Development assistance per capita:	$9.88
Literacy rate:	12%
International affiliations:	UN, Group of 77
Defence expenditure:	$379m.

Laos, a former French possession independent since 1949, lies in the shape of an irregular key-hole, landlocked in South-East Asia. There is a long eastern frontier with Vietnam, Cambodia to the South, Thailand to the south-west, Burma to the north-west and China to the north. The country is covered in dense jungle and the mountains in the north rise over 2 700 m. The climate is monsoonal with rain from May to September (up to 375 cm in the south); continuously high humidity, temperatures 57–93°F. The capital, Vientiane, with 120 000 inhabitants, is on the Thai border. The country is extremely underdeveloped, largely because of twenty years of fighting, which culminated in a communist victory. A high level of imports (including rice) has made foreign aid essential. Development priorities are agricultural self-sufficiency, infrastructure and hydro-electric energy.

Natural resources: Tin, timber
Crops: Rice, maize, tobacco, coffee, cotton, opium; insufficient irrigation, mechanization, planting, distribution; collectivization resisted.
Animals: Cattle, buffalo, goats, sheep, poultry
Forestry: Two-thirds of land, but transport problems; teak is exploited with the use of elephants and floated on the Mekong River.
Agriculture: 85% of the population is engaged in subsistence farming on less than 10% of land.
Industry: Mining, timber; 600 small factories built in late 1970s for animal feed, vaccines, agricultural tools and machinery, textiles, bricks. Priority for vehicle repairs (to ease distribution problems); hydro-electricity supplies Vientiane and is being developed.
Exports: Timber, tin, cotton (all via Thailand)
Imports: Food, petrol (pipeline from Vietnam) manufactures,

agricultural machinery
Partners: Thailand, Japan, aid from USSR and China
Education: 600 000 pupils in 1979; growing
Communications: Poor; no railway; 3 000 km of all-weather roads

Lebanon

Population:	2.8m.
GNP:	$2.9bn.
Growth rate per capita:	n/a
Development assistance per capita:	$8.92
Literacy rate:	86%
International affiliations:	UN, Arab League, Group of 77, N/A
Defence expenditure:	$286m.

Lebanon, a French mandated territory from 1919 to 1943, lies on the eastern shore of the Mediterranean, almost surrounded by Syria but with a short southern border with Israel. The country was the commercial centre of the Middle East with two-thirds of its GNP deriving from commercial services, principally banking. Civil war between the Moslems and Christians (the population is evenly split) from 1975–6 destroyed the capital, Beirut, leaving only 10% of industry functioning. The government's priority is reconstruction as a basis for reconciliation between the two communities. Lebanon is 216 km long by 32–56 km wide with the high Lebanese mountains running down the centre. 64% of the land is desert, waste or urban. Humidity is high; temperatures do not exceed 90°F.

Natural resources: Iron ore
Crops: Fruit, wheat, corn, barley, potatoes, tobacco, olives, onions; food imports necessary
Animals: Goats, sheep, cattle, camels, hogs
Agriculture: 60% of population, 27% of land. Bad soil erosion; irrigation problems
Industry: Service industries, food processing, textiles, cement, oil-refining (oil from Iraq and Saudi Arabia); mainly small-scale and around Beirut
Exports: Fruit, vegetables, textiles
Imports: Metals, machinery, food

Partners: Saudi Arabia, Kuwait, Syria, Libya, Iraq; USA, EEC
Education: Large number of state and private schools, the former mainly primary; 6 universities, centre for whole Middle East

Lesotho

Population:	931 000
GDP per capita:	$138
Growth rate per capita:	8.5%
Development assistance per capita:	$30.94
Literacy rate:	40%
International affiliations:	UN, OAU, CW, ACP, South African Customs Union, Group of 77, N/A
Defence expenditure:	n/a

Lesotho, a former British colony independent since 1966, lies landlocked within South Africa with the Orange Free State to the west and north, Natal to the east and Cape Province to the south. The country is dependent upon South Africa not only for trade but also for the employment of its population in mining, farming and industry. The main activity is subsistence agriculture. Three-quarters of the country is highland rising to 3 300 m and the western quarter is lowland, generally unfertile. Soil erosion is being fought by mechanical digging of graded furrows (terracing) and by tree-planting. Land is generally inalienable, being held by the King in trust for the nation.

Natural resource: Diamonds
Crops: Summer-maize, sorghum, beans; winter-wheat, peas, barley, oats
Animals: Sheep, goats, cattle; new poultry plant at Maseru, the capital (pop. 45 000)
Industry: Carpets, woollen clothes, candles, pottery, tractor assembly, grain mills; new industrial zone at Ficksburg Bridge; tourism growing
Exports: Wool, mohair, cattle, diamonds
Imports: Manufactures, food, machinery, livestock, vehicles, tobacco
Partners: South Africa; Customs Union of Lesotho, Botswana, Swaziland and South Africa

Education: 232 000 pupils mainly at mission schools; not compulsory but 75% of children get some education before the age of 20; boys are needed for herding from 8–14; National University of Lesotho at Roma, near Maseru
Communications: Extensive horse-trails, pack-animals needed; 200 km paved road; rail link to South Africa

Liberia

Population:	1.8m.
GNP:	$665m.
Growth rate per capita:	1.5%
Development assistance per capita:	$15.49
Literacy rate:	24%
International affiliations:	UN, OAU, ACP, ECOWAS, Group of 77, N/A
Defence expenditure:	$16.5m.

Liberia, the first independent republic in Africa (1847), was founded by freed slaves on the south-west coast of West Africa. Sierra Leone lies to the north along the coast and Guinea inland; to the east is the Ivory Coast. Only 5% of the population is descended from freed slaves but they form the dominant group despite a policy of integration with the indigenous peoples. The economy depends on the world prices for iron ore, rubber and timber. Government has been very centralized and in March 1980 there was a military coup, prompted by economic decline and complaints of corruption. Traditionally, foreign investment has been encouraged and successfully attracted. The capital, Monrovia, with a population of 208 000, is one of four main ports. Tropical rainforest covers the country. Rain up to 500 cm on the coast.

Natural resources: Iron ore, rubber, timber, diamonds; resources not completely surveyed
Crops: Rice, cassava, coffee, cocoa, sugar (developed in association with China)
Animals: Cattle, pigs, sheep, poultry
Forestry: Rubber (Firestone and other multinationals run plantations and are biggest employers in Liberia), oil-palm; timber (grew rapidly in mid-1970s)
Agriculture: 75% of work-force, 20% of land
Industry: Processing iron ore, diamonds, rubber and food;

oil-mill (for palm-oil)

Exports: Iron ore (72% in 1976), rubber, timber, diamonds
Imports: Machinery, petroleum products, vehicles, food, manufactures
Partners: EEC, USA
Education: 238 000 pupils in compulsory education from 6–16 at state and mission schools; University of Liberia
Communications: 7 200 km of road but tracks only in interior where porters necessary. Rain damages roads. Iron ore railway. Ship registration is easy and cheap.

Libya

Population:	2.93m.
GNP:	$19bn.
Growth rate per capita:	– 0.4%
Development assistance per capita:	$3.15
Literacy rate:	35%
International affiliations:	UN, Arab League, OAU, OPEC, OAPEC, Group of 77, N/A
Defence expenditure:	$448m.

For most of its history, Libya has been ruled by foreigners, most recently by a joint British–French administration before independence in 1951. The country lies in the centre of North Africa with a long Mediterranean coastline, Egypt to the east, Sudan to the south-east, Chad and Niger to the south, Algeria and Tunisia to the west. 92% of the land is desert or semi-desert. Cultivation is confined to the coastal strip, two small hilly areas near the coast and inland oases. Humidity is generally high, rain very little and in spring and autumn the south wind (*ghibi*) from the desert brings heat and dust. 90% of the population live on 10% of the land and 44% are under 15. Oil is the basis for development; 15% of revenues are always reserved and 70% of the rest is spent in infrastructure, health, education, welfare, housing and industry. The government seeks greater equality of income, increased state control of the economy and freedom from foreign influence, as well as Arab union. The capital, Tripoli, on the western part of the coast, has 281 000 inhabitants.

Natural resources: Natural gas, petroleum

Crops: Cereals, dates, olives, peanuts, citrus fruits
Animals: Sheep, goats, cattle: nomadic herding; poultry
Agriculture: 20% of work-force, 7% of land (N.B. plan to reclaim and develop land)
Industry: Crude oil, processing food, textiles, paper, soap, cement
Exports: Crude oil (90%)
Imports: Machinery, manufactures, food
Partners: Italy, West Germany, USA, France, UK
Education: 667 000 school-children; 13 000 students; two universities
Communications: Mostly by road; well-paved road from Tunis to Egypt

Madagascar

Population:	8.68m.
GNP:	$3.32bn.
Growth rate per capita:	− 2.1%
Development assistance per capita:	$8.59
Literacy rate:	40%
International affiliations:	UN, OAU, ACP, Group of 77, N/A
Defence expenditure:	$102m.

Madagascar, a former French Protectorate independent since 1960, is the largest island in the world (1 568 km by 576 km), lying in the Indian Ocean 400 km off the coast of Mozambique. The interior is a high plateau (750–1 950 m) and the south is arid. The highlands are temperate and the coast tropical with monsoon rain on the east coast. Cyclones frequently cause damage. The economy is essentially agricultural and development is aimed at increasing agricultural productivity by establishing distributive co-operatives and *fokonola* communes. The government, dominated by the Merina people from the central highlands, seeks de-centralized public control of the economy to replace traditional ownership by French, Indian and Chinese minorities. The capital, Antananarivo, has 400 000 inhabitants.

Natural resources: Graphite, chrome, coal, bauxite, tar sands, semi-precious stones, gold
Crops: Rice, coffee, vanilla, sugar, cloves, cotton, sisal,

groundnuts, tobacco, pepper
Animals: 9 million cattle, pigs, sheep, goats, poultry
Forestry: Valuable woods, notably gums and resins
Agriculture: 83% of work-force, 58% of land-pasture, 5% of land cultivated
Industry: Processed food, textiles, mining, paper, oil refining, vehicle assembly. Recent developments: TV, radio, bicycles, plastics, paints, metals, chemicals
Exports: Coffee, cloves, vanilla, textiles
Imports: Machinery, chemicals, crude oil, rice, metals, mineral products, food
Partners: France, USA
Education: Compulsory from 6–14; half-million primary pupils, 105 000 secondary, 5 600 students at University of Antananarivo
Communications: 40 000 km of roads for motor vehicles

Malawi

Population:	6.0m.
GNP:	$1.266bn.
Growth rate per capita:	4.1%
Development assistance per capita:	$13.07
Literacy rate:	25%
International affiliations:	UN, OAU, CW, ACP, World Bank, Group of 77
Defence expenditure:	$61.7m.

Malawi, formerly the British Protectorate of Nyasaland, independent in 1964, lies down the western shore of Lake Malawi in south-east Africa. The southern part is surrounded by Mozambique; Zambia to the west, Tanzania to the north-east. Malawi measures 832 km (north-east) by 80–160 km. Blantyre, the commercial centre (pop. 229 000), lies in the south and the population density declines as one goes north. The capital, Lilongwe (pop. 103 000), is in the centre of the country. Although there are few natural resources, Malawi has followed a well-planned course of development and is almost self-sufficient in agriculture. Amongst other projects there is the National Rural Development Project (1977–97), road-building, the Tedzini barrage project and the Nkula hydro-electric project. Real growth has averaged 6.5% since independence.

Natural resources: Limestone, marble
Crops: Cash: tobacco, tea, sugar, groundnuts. Food: maize, rice, millet, cassava
Animals: Cattle, sheep, goats, pigs
Forestry and Fishery: Originally wood unsuitable for joinery, but softwood planted in the 1950s; new plantings; fish are a vital part of Malawians' diet
Agriculture: 90% of work-force, 30% of land, 46% of GDP
Industry: Food, drink, tobacco, textiles, footwear; mainly indigenous materials
Exports: Tobacco, tea, sugar, groundnuts (together 89%)
Partners: UK, South Africa, USA, West Germany, Japan, Netherlands
Education: Not compulsory. 690 000 pupils; 1 100 students at University of Malawi
Communications: 2 880 km of main road, railways to ports in Mozambique

Malaysia

Population:	13.6m
GNP:	$14.9bn.
Growth rate per capita:	4.9%
Development assistance per capita:	$5.95
Literacy rate:	50%, 25% in the east
International affiliations:	UN, ADB, ASEAN, CW, Colombo Plan, Group of 77, N/A
Defence expenditure:	$1.47bn.

The Federation of Malaysia was established in 1963, bringing together a number of former British colonies including Singapore, which withdrew in 1965. The Federation consists of two main parts: (1) the states of Western Malaysia (Peninsular Malaysia) which occupy the Malay peninsular, south of Thailand, separated from Sumatra by the Straits of Malacca; (2) Eastern Malaysia, comprising Sarawak and Sabah on the north coast of the island of Borneo, the southern part of which is in Indonesia. Between them lies the South China Sea. The economy is strong with rising investment and production, led by the public sector but attractive also to private capital. From 1971–75 growth averaged 7.4% with agriculture in the lead. The 3rd 5-year plan (1976–80) envisaged an attack on poverty with an emphasis on regional development. Unemployment was 7% in 1975; targets are 6.1% (1980) and 3.6% (1990). Exports rose by 22% a year from 1976–78 and rural income has increased. Most of the population live in Western Malaysia and 45% are under 15. The capital, Kuala Lumpur (pop. 500 000) is in the west of Western Malaysia.

Natural resources: Tin, oil, copper, timber
Crops: Rubber, palm-oil, cocoa, rice, pepper, coconut. (Rice grows in the west and is sent to the east.)
Animals: Cattle, buffaloes, sheep, pigs, goats
Forestry: Hardwoods, pine, plywood, veneer
Agriculture: 59% of work-force, 12% of land, 30% of GNP, 55% of exports
Industry: Steel, vehicles, electronics, petroleum, tourism
Exports: Rubber, tin, timber, palm-oil (exports are worth more than half of GNP.)
Imports: Machinery, vehicles, chemicals, manufactures
Partners: Japan, UK, USA
Education: Free 6 years primary, 3 years secondary; 5 universities
Health: Campaign against malaria and tuberculosis has been successful.

Mali

Population:	6.55m.
GNP:	$839m.
Growth rate per capita:	1.3%
Development assistance per capita:	$17.36
Literacy rate:	less than 5%
International affiliations:	UN, OAU, ACP, African Development Bank, Group of 77, N/A
Defence expenditure:	$33.4m

Mali lies landlocked in the centre of West Africa, a former French colony surrounded by former French colonies: Mauritania and Senegal to the west, Guinea, Ivory Coast and Upper Volta to the south, Niger to the east and Algeria to the north. The northern part of the country is in the Sahara desert, the southern part savanna, watered by the River Niger. The capital, Bamako (pop. 200 000), is in the south-west. Agriculture is supplemented by food-processing industry but growth has been hampered and even reversed by severe droughts. There is little foreign investment. Plans to improve agriculture include an irrigation scheme centred on a barrage at Sansanding.

Natural resources: Iron ore, bauxite, uranium, copper, gold – known but unexploited; salt
Crops: Sorghum, millet, rice – subsistence; cotton, groundnuts – cash
Animals: Cattle, goats, sheep – many lost in 1972 drought. Fishing in Niger River
Agriculture: 50% of land, 90% of population, 50% GDP, 100% of exports
Industry: Food-processing, textiles; 11% of GDP, 1% of population
Exports: Meat, live animals, cotton, fish, groundnuts, gum, dried fish, skins
Imports: Food, machinery, vehicles, petroleum products, chemicals, textiles
Partners: EEC, especially France; Communist countries, Ivory Coast
Education: 15% of the 6–14 age group attend school
Communications: 14 000 km roads (50% all-weather); steamboats on River Niger

Mauritania

Population:	1.61m.
GNP:	$320m.
Growth rate per capita:	– 1.9%
Development assistance per capita:	$37.04
Literacy rate:	10%
International affiliations:	UN, OAU, Arab League, ACP, Group of 77, N/A
Defence expenditure:	$29m.

Mauritania, formerly a French colony, is in north-west Africa; Senegal to the south, Mali to south and east, Algeria to north-east, the former Spanish Sahara to north-west, the Atlantic Ocean to the west. The southern part of the coastal plain favours agriculture. Nouakchott, the capital (pop. 120 000), is in this region. Inland, the land rises and is drier; in the north lies the Sahara desert and mountains. For half the year the daytime temperature exceeds 100°F, although the nights are cool. There are virtually two separate economies; traditional subsistence agriculture and herding and the modern sector dominated by iron ore. Since iron ore was first exported in 1963 the GNP has more than doubled and exports quintupled. Mauritania is a member of the Sahel Development Project which aims at food self-sufficiency for Sahel states. Government expenditure is increasing, partly because a third of Spanish Sahara is now administered as part of Mauritania.

Natural resources: Iron ore, copper, gypsum; oil exploration under way
Crops: Cereals, dates
Animals: Sheep, goats, cattle, donkeys, horses, camels; 1969–73 drought 75% losses
Agriculture: 90% population, 5% land; extensive fishing
Industry: Iron and copper-ore processing, gypsum, fish-processing
Exports: Iron ore, fish products, livestock marketed in Senegal and Mali, gum arabic
Imports: Sugar, cast iron, steel, transport equipment
Partners: France, UK, USA, Spain, Italy, West Germany, Japan, Senegal
Communications: 6 000 km of road; only 500 km tarred. Deep-water port project at Nouakchott

Mauritius

Population:	0.91m.
GNP:	$873
Growth rate per capita:	6.3%
Development assistance per capita:	$24.03
Literacy rate:	61%
International affiliations:	UN, CW, OAU, OCAM, ACP, Group of 77, N/A
Defence expenditure:	n/a

The small, densely populated island of Mauritius became independent from the UK in 1968. A volcanic island with coral reefs, in the Indian Ocean, north of the Tropic of Capricorn and 800 km east of Madagascar. The economy is dominated by sugar but despite price stability under the Lomé Convention, the government seeks diversification and development of industry. Cyclones occasionally devastate crops. The population is of varied descent: 67% Indian, 28% Creole, 3% Chinese and 2% French; the last group dominant in commercial life. Unemployment is a major problem. Capital: Port Louis (pop. 138 000).

Crops: Sugar, tea, tobacco, rice, aloe, potatoes, onions
Animals: Cattle, goats, poultry
Agriculture: 60% of land, 29% work-force
Industry: Sugar – 89% of foreign exchange; consumer goods produced in 'Export Processing Zones', areas with tax advantages
Partners: UK, USA, South Africa, Canada, Australia
Educations: 90% of primary school-age children attend; free, voluntary
Communications: Good – 9½ miles motorway, 561 km main road; new airport at Plaine des Roches

Mexico

Population:	71.5m.
GNP:	$91bn.
Growth rate per capita:	1.0%
Development assistance per capita:	$0.93
Literacy rate:	65%
International affiliations:	UN, OAS, LAFTA, Seabeds Committee
Defence expenditure:	$518m.

Mexico, the largest state in Latin America after Brazil, lies south of the USA bounded by the Pacific Ocean to the west and south, the Gulf of Mexico to the east and Belize and Guatemala to the south-east. Mexico proclaimed independence from Spain in 1810 and the present policy derives from the Revolution of 1910. The topography is a mixture of coastal jungle, desert plains, high plateaux and mountains and the climate is generally hot and dry. Since the second world war economic development has been substantial but the 1970s were dominated by financial problems and very high levels of unemployment. As a result of 50 years of agrarian reform, much land is in the hands of subsistence farmers whose productivity the government seeks to enhance by forming co-operatives and whose income it supports by intervention. Most enterprises require Mexican control but foreign investment is encouraged in export products, import substitution, depressed regions and labour-intensive activities. The capital, Mexico City, has a population of 7 million. In 1974 the UN General Assembly approved the Charter of the Economic Rights and Duties of States, an initiative launched by Mexican President Echeverria in 1972.

Natural resources: Oil, silver, lead, zinc, copper, gold, gas, sulphur, coal, timber
Crops: Maize, cotton, wheat, coffee, sugar-cane; 12% land
Animals: 29 million cattle; 8 million sheep; hogs, goats, mules, donkeys, horses; 40% land
Forestry: Controlled exploitation of hard and softwoods; 22% of land
Agriculture: 40% work-force, 9.7% GDP
Industry: Food-processing, chemicals, metals, oil products, cement, aluminium, synthetic fibres: 29.9% GDP
Exports: Oil, coffee, sugar, cotton, tomatoes, fruits, sisal, sulphur
Imports: Machinery, vehicles, tools, iron and steel products, cereals
Partners: USA, West Germany, Japan, France, UK
Education: Compulsory 6–14, 72% attendance; 25% attendance 15–19; 507 higher educational institutions including universities
Communications: 208 000 km roads (116 000 km surfaced), 32 000 km railways; 49 ports

Mongolia

Population:	1.7m.
GNP:	$2.8bn.
Growth rate per capita:	n/a
Development assistance per capita:	n/a
Literacy rate:	80%
International affiliations:	UN, Comecon
Defence expenditure:	$127m.

Mongolia, sometimes called Outer Mongolia, lies in the heart of central Asia between the USSR and China. The country was originally united by Genghis Khan in 1203 and has been occupied by China and Japan at different times. Nearly all the land is above 300m; from the Gobi Desert in the south-east the land rises through prairies to high mountains and uncontrollable northern rivers. The economy is strongly tied to the economy of the USSR; there is a common electrical power system, and Russian workers make up for labour shortages. The traditional nomadic, pastoral way of life persists but the tent-dwellers are now highly organized in production units with social and economic centres in permanent buildings. The population is becoming more sedentary and mechanized agriculture is growing. The 7th 5-year-plan (1981–85) emphasizes state-farms, extension of arable farming, mining and house-building. Previous plans have suffered from labour shortages and climatic conditions (blizzards) as well as ingrained resistance to change. The capital, Ulaanbaatar, has a population of 300 000.

Natural resources: Coal, copper, molybdenum; gold, uranium reported; oil from Gobi Desert stopped
Crops: Wheat, oats, barley
Animals: Cattle, horses, pigs, poultry, bees
Agriculture: Land 1% arable; virgin land being tilled also; 84% pasture and wasteland
Industry: Animal products – meat, butter, wool, hair, fur, hides; building materials; tourism
Exports: Livestock, animal products, metal ores, coal
Imports: Machinery and equipment, processed food, consumer goods, sugar, tea, building materials
Partners: USSR and Comecon, Japan
Education: 4 years compulsory (7 in population centres); 23 000 students (1977) in higher education

Morocco

Population:	20m.
GNP:	$15.2bn.
Growth rate per capita:	3.8%
Development assistance per capita:	$10.06
Literacy rate:	24% male, 15% female
International affiliations:	UN, OAU, Arab League, Group of 77, N/A
Defence expenditure:	$676m.

Morocco, a French protectorate from 1912 to 1956, lies on the north-west coast of Africa. The 1950 km coastline faces the Mediterranean, the Straits of Gibraltar and the Atlantic Ocean. To the south-east is Algeria, to the south the former Spanish Sahara which Morocco has partitioned with Mauritania. The capital, Rabat, and Casablanca, the commercial centre, are in the north-western coastal plain where most people live. Inland are the Atlas mountains and in the south and south-east the Sahara desert. In the early 1970s Morocco seemed set for rapid industrialization and development built on rising phosphate earnings, but world recession in the late 1970s reduced demand, forced the dropping of ambitious plans and increased borrowing. Bad harvests aggravated the situation. Development continues to be accompanied by import restrictions and cramped by defence spending of 17.5% GNP.

Natural resources: Phosphates (70% world reserves), iron, manganese, lead, fisheries; some crude oil
Crops: Barley, wheat, fruit, figs, olives, vegetables, sugarbeets
Animals: Camels, horses, cattle, pigs, sheep, goats, poultry
Forestry: Acacia and eucalyptus for tanning, cork, cedar, pine cyprus
Fishery: Abundant – tunny-fish, mackerel, sardines, anchovies
Agriculture: 70% population, 25% GDP, 33% exports
Industry: Mining, textiles, fish-processing, paper, vehicle assembly, light consumer goods, chemicals, tourism
Exports: Unrefined phosphate, phosphoric acid, citrus fruits, vegetables, canned food including fish, carpets
Imports: Capital goods, fuel, food, consumer goods
Partners: France, Italy, West Germany, Spain, USA
Education: Compulsory from 7–13, attendance 42%; 6 universities, students from Africa and Middle East
Communications: 52000km of roads (22000 surfaced), 17000km rail; free port of Tangier; deep-water port planned at Jarf Lasfar

Mozambique

Population:	10.17m.
GNP:	$16bn.
Growth rate per capita:	– 4.4%
Development assistance per capita:	$5.97
Literacy rate:	20%
International affiliations:	UN, OAU, Group of 77, N/A

Defence expenditure: $177m.

Mozambique obtained independence from Portugal in 1975. The country lies on the south-east coast of Africa, south of Tanzania, north of South Africa; to the west, Zimbabwe, to the north-west Malawi. Half of the country is coastal lowland; inland the land rises to mountains on the western frontier. The lowland climate is subtropical, the rain variable with resulting floods and droughts. The economy is weak and under-developed. Most people live on subsistence agriculture. There is a small amount of industry but the imports necessary to sustain and develop it depend upon unreliable cash crop export earnings. Raw materials, skilled labour and credit are low. Foreign property and several service sectors have been nationalized. The government receives gold from South Africa for providing mineworkers. The capital, Maputo, has a population of 384 000.

Natural resources: Coal iron, beryl, copper, ore relatively unexploited
Crops: Cotton, tobacco, cashew nuts, sugar, tea, copra, sisal, cereals
Agriculture: 80% population, 30% land
Industry: Food-processing, oil-refining, textiles, beverages, chemicals, tobacco, cement (around Maputo there are steel and engineering works); 5% population
Exports: Cashew nuts, cotton, coal, petrol, molasses, sugar, copra, tea
Imports: Machinery, vehicles, metal, petroleum products, textiles
Partners: Portugal, South Africa, USA; diversifying to other African states and Communist countries
Education: Efforts to improve schooling and adult literacy but teacher shortage. University in Maputo
Communications: 3 200 km of railway; ports – Maputo, Beira; mainly east–west to service South Africa, Botswana, Zimbabwe, Zambia, Zaire and Malawi; brings in foreign exchange to pay for transport; north–south road being built

Nepal
Population: 14m.
GNP: $1.76bn.
Growth rate per capita: 1.5%

Development assistance per capita:	$4.34
Literacy rate:	16%
International affiliations:	UN, Colombo Plan, Group of 77, N/A
Defence expenditure:	$19m.

Nepal lies on the southern slopes of the Himalayas in central Asia, 800 km east-to-west by 160 km north–south. To the west, south and east – India; to the north the Tibetan region of China. The country is formed of 3 east–west zones, the southern *Terai*, part of the Ganges plain, the central hill country and the Himalayas including Mt. Everest, the highest mountain in the world at 8 700 m. Nepal has developed greatly since 1951 when there were virtually no public services, power supplies and communications and only rudimentary administration. Agriculture is still the main activity but under five development plans (until 1980) transport, communication, industry, administration and land reform have been developed; trade has increased and hydro-electricity serves much of the country and is exported to India. The King has established a non-party hierarcy of councils (*panchayat*) rooted in village life. The capital, Kathmandu (pop. 150 000), is in the hill country.

Natural resources: Water, timber, coal; copper, iron, mica, zinc and cobalt reserves
Crops: Paddy rice, wheat, jute
Animals: Cattle (including buffaloes), goats, hogs, poultry
Agriculture: Land – 30% cultivated, 33% forest; population – 94%; GDP – 66%
Industry: Food-processing, jute and sugar mills; match, leather, cigarette and shoe factories; chemical works, tourism, industrial estates at Patan and Balaju
Exports: Food grains, jute, timber, oilseeds, ghee (clarified butter), potatoes, hides and skins
Imports: Textiles, cigarettes, salt, petrol, paraffin, sugar, machinery, medicine, footwear, paper, cement, iron and steel, tea
Education: Many schools built; new Tribhuvan University (1960)
Communications: Road links to Tibet and India; east–west highway nearly complete; but some areas only accessible by foot

Nicaragua

Population:	2.5m.
GNP:	$2bn.
Growth rate per capita:	0.7%
Development assistance per capita:	$17.58
Literacy rate:	46%
International affiliations:	UN, OAS, Group of 77
Defence expenditure:	$3.3m.

The largest central American republic, with Caribbean and Pacific coasts, Honduras to the north and Costa Rica to the south. Nicaragua was a Spanish colony until 1820 and became separately independent in 1838. The country hit the headlines in 1980 when the Sandinista guerrillas overthrew the Somoza régime; it is too early to gauge the effect of new policies on development. The Pacific coastal plain containing the capital, Managua (pop. 463 000), and the marshy Caribbean coast are separated by mountains, woods and hills. Development is restricted by the lack of resources and infrastructure. Managua was destroyed by an earthquake in 1972 and severely damaged during fighting in 1980.

Natural resources: Gold, silver, copper; tungsten deposits found; off-shore oil exploration
Crops: Cotton, coffee, sugar, cocoa; also bananas – recovering from blight
Agriculture: 30% of land, 65% population, 22% GDP
Industry: Food-processing, drinks, textiles, chemical, petroleum and metal products
Exports: Cotton, coffee, beef, chemical products, sugar
Imports: Machines and vehicles, chemicals, crude oil, food
Partners: USA, Japan, West Germany, Costa Rica, Guatemala, Venezuela

Niger

Population:	5.4m.
GNP:	$1.5bn.
Growth rate per capita:	−0.1%
Development assistance per capita:	$25.62

Literacy rate:	6%
International affiliations:	UN, West African Economic Community, OAU, ACP, N/A
Defence expenditure:	$23.4m

Niger, a former French colony (independent 1960), lies on the southern edge of the Sahara Desert in the centre of northern Africa. To the east Chad; to the south Nigeria and Benin; to the south-west Upper Volta; to the west Mali; to the north Algeria and Libya. 80% of the country is desert. Agriculture is largely confined to the Niger River valley in the south-west, where the capital, Niamey, is found. The rest of the country is savanna where livestock are raised and a nomadic life-style preserved. Development is obstructed by extreme water scarcity which reached the level of a major disaster in 1973 after five dry years; food production dropped and livestock perished. The transport of goods for export via Benin and Nigeria is prohibitively expensive. The current 10-year-plan ends in 1982; the government aims to diversify food, improve infrastructure and develop water supplies.

Natural resources: Uranium, coal, iron, salt, tin, limestone, gypsum; oil not yet found
Crops: Millet, sorghum, beans and rice for food; groundnuts, cotton and gum arabic for sale
Animals: Horses, cattle, sheep, goats, asses, camels, cattle regarded as status symbols, not income
Agriculture: 3% land (plus pasture); 90% population
Industry: Textiles, cement, processing of agricultural products; uranium processing
Exports: Groundnuts, uranium, livestock, gum arabic. Animals are driven across frontiers, without official records.
Imports: Fuel, machinery, vehicles, consumer goods
Education: 12% attendance; primary education on TV in Niamey; 782 students at university in 1978
Communications: Poor roads – 2 650 km tarred. No railway

Nigeria

| Population: | 76.4m. |
| GNP: | $35bn. |

Growth rate per capita:	4.3%
Development assistance per capita:	$0.90
Literacy rate:	25%
International affiliations:	UN, OAU, CW, OPEC, ECOWAS, ACP, Group of 77, N/A
Defence expenditure	$1.7bn.

Nigeria obtained independence from the UK in 1960. Civil war followed the attempted secession of Biafra from 1967 to 1970. The country lies on the south coast of West Africa with Benin to the west, Niger to the north, Chad to the north-west and Cameroon to the east. The coast is humid and hot; 96 km inland there is rainforest and in the centre of the country a high, dry, plateau; in the extreme north the desert encroaches. The reconstruction of the country since the civil war has been based upon oil revenues. Light and heavy industry is growing and the government has invested strongly in infrastructure.

Natural resources: Petroleum, natural gas, tin, columbite, iron-ore, coal, limestone, lead, zinc, gold, uranium
Crops: Cocoa, rubber, palm-oil, yams, groundnuts, cotton, soybean, millet, sorghum, corn, rice
Animals: Cattle, sheep, goats, pigs, poultry
Agriculture: 30% of land, 70% of work-force
Industry: Cotton, rubber, petroleum, textiles, cement, food, metal, timber, vehicle assembly; nascent iron and steel industry. Natural gas and hydro-electric power station
Exports: Petroleum (93%), tin, coal, columbite, cocoa, palm-oil, rubber
Imports: Machinery, vehicles, food, manufactured goods
Partners: UK, USA, France, West Germany, Netherlands, Japan, Netherlands Antilles
Education: Primary education free and compulsory (6–12); free tuition at 15 universities with more planned
Health: Successful medical campaigns but big problems with tropical diseases including blindness, yaws, leprosy and sleeping sickness
Communications: 80 000 km of road; 3 500 km of rail; roads and bridges under construction

Oman

Population:	0.93m.
GNP:	$2.55bn.
Growth rate per capita:	2.6%
Development assistance per capita:	$5.70
Literacy rate:	10%
International affiliations:	UN, Arab League, IBRD, IMF, Group of 77, N/A
Defence expenditure:	$879m.

This small oil-rich state occupies the south-eastern corner of Arabia and was in the early nineteenth century the greatest state in the Arabian peninsular, with possessions in East Africa including Zanzibar, and great wealth as a centre of the arms and slave trades. Present prosperity is derived from oil found in 1964 and new finds in 1975 and 1979. The oil should outlast the twentieth century but Oman faces severe problems of disease, poverty and illiteracy. The oil is jointly owned by the Sultan and foreign oil companies.

Natural resources: Oil, asbestos, marble, copper, limestone, chrome, manganese, iron
Crops: Dates, limes, alfalfa, vegetables, fruit, tobacco; irrigation required
Animals: Cattle, sheep, goats, camels
Agriculture: 83% of work-force, 0.2% of land
Industry: Petroleum, fish, construction
Exports: Oil, dates, limes, dried fish, tobacco
Imports: Machinery, vehicles, food, animals, fuel, tobacco
Partners: Japan, UK, United Arab Emirates, West Germany, USA
Education: Many schools built in the 1970s; 30% attendance – two-thirds of pupils are boys. No university
Communications: Modern airport at Seeb; deep-water port at Matrah; rapid road programme – 1 272 km of paved road at end of 1976

Pakistan

Population:	82.7m.
GNP:	$18.5bn.

Growth rate per capita:	0.9%
Development assistance per capita:	$6.51
Literacy rate:	17%
International affiliations:	UN, ADB, IDA, Colombo Plan, Group of 77
Defence expenditure:	$1.18bn.

In 1947 British India was partitioned and the Muslim country of Pakistan was created. In 1971 after civil war the eastern part seceded to become Bangladesh. The territory of Pakistan today straddles the Indus Valley. The eastern plain runs down to the north-west frontier of India and the mountains and desert of the west cross into Iran in the south and Afghanistan in the north. Despite the huge irrigation system based on the Indus, agricultural productivity has been low because of floods, droughts and pest, under-investment and (until 1977) absentee landlords. Land reform, government provision of fertilizer, the introduction of high-yield seeds and the reclamation of desert and saline areas are improving the situation. The emphasis is on rural development with a policy of high agricultural prices to strengthen the rural community.

Natural resources: Natural gas, petroleum (15% of domestic consumption), coal, iron ore
Crops: Wheat, cotton, rice, maize, sugar-cane, fruit, dates
Animals: Cattle, buffaloes, sheep, goats, poultry
Agriculture: 24% of land, 59% of work-force, 45% of national income
Industry: Cotton textiles, food-processing, tobacco, engineering, chemicals, gas, electric power (and nuclear reactor at Islamabad)
Exports: Rice, cotton, yarn, textiles, light manufactures
Imports: Capital goods, raw materials, food grains, consumer goods
Partners: USA, Japan, UK, West Germany, Hong Kong, Saudi Arabia
Education: The principle of free, compulsory education at primary level is accepted with targets of 1982 and 1987 for 100% attendance by boys and girls respectively. There are 15 universities and a TV and radio adult literacy campaign.
Communications: 31 000 km of roads, including Karakoran Highway to China; 9 000 km of railways

Panama

Population:	1.8m.
GDP per capita:	$1 250
Growth rate per capita:	-0.1%
Development assistance per capita:	$21.51
Literacy rate:	82%
International affiliations:	UN, OAS, IMF, IDB, Group of 77, N/A
Defence expenditure:	(11 000 men)

Panama was discovered by Columbus in 1501, became independent from Spain in 1821 and from Colombia in 1903. In 1979 the republic resumed sovereignty over the canal zone, which passes through the centre joining the Caribbean and the Pacific. The country forms an isthmus connecting North and South America, represented immediately by Costa Rica to the west and Colombia to the east. The economy is in two separate parts. Half the population pursue moneyless subsistence agriculture and the other half live on the commerce generated by the canal. As well as producing a fixed income from the USA, the canal has stimulated the development of trade services and banking. The capital, Panama City, lies on the Pacific Coast and has a population of 467 000.

Natural resources: Copper
Crops: Bananas, maize, sugar, rice
Animals: Cattle, pigs, poultry
Agriculture: 29.3% of land (57% of which is pasture), 40% of work-force
Industry: Oil-refining, sugar, cigarettes, clothes, food-processing, shoes, soap, cement
Exports: Bananas, refined oil, sugar, shrimps
Imports: Crude oil, capital goods, food (60% of food is imported)
Partners: USA, Ecuador, Venezuela, Japan, Saudi Arabia, West Germany, Italy
Education: Free and compulsory 7–15; two universities
Communications: Main highway is part of the Pan-American Highway linking North and South America; a railway runs alongside the canal.

Papua New Guinea

Population:	3.2m.
GNP:	$1.9bn.
Growth rate per capita:	2.2%
Development assistance per capita:	$94.56
Literacy rate:	33%
International affiliations:	UN, IBRD, ADB, ACP, CW, Colombo Plan, Group of 77
Defence expenditure:	$28.2m.

After a mixed colonial history going back to the sixteenth century, the combined territories of Papua and New Guinea became independent in 1975. The country is comprised of the eastern part of the island of New Guinea together with smaller islands to the north-east, lying within 10 degrees south of the Equator in the South Pacific. The western part of the main island is in Indonesia and Australia is to the south. The main island has a mountainous interior and swampy coastal plains. The majority of the people live in communities of a few hundred, often totally isolated from and ignorant of close neighbours. 80% of the population is engaged in subsistence agriculture but the government is developing light import-substituting industries. Mineral exports are valuable and debt-servicing requires only 5% of export earnings. The capital, Port Moresby, in the south-east, has a population of 117 000. There is some movement of labour to urban areas.

Natural resources: Copper, gold, silver, natural gas, timber, tuna
Crops: Sweet potatoes, sugar, taro, root crops, coffee, copra, palm oil, cocoa, tea, rubber
Animals: Cattle, pigs, goats, poultry
Industry: Processing of palm oil, copra, coffee, timber, tea, beer, soap, concrete, clothes, paper, metal, household goods
Imports: Food, machinery, vehicles, manufactures, fuels, chemicals
Exports: Copper, gold, silver, coffee, cocoa, copra, palm oil, timber
Partners: Japan, Australia, USA, West Germany, Spain, Singapore, UK
Education: There are primary, secondary, technical and vocational schools; two universities – 3 000 students in 1977

Communications: 19 000 km of roads but much of the interior is inaccessible.

Paraguay

Population:	3.3m.
GNP:	$2.14bn.
Growth rate per capita:	4.5%
Development assistance per capita:	$15.48
Literacy rate:	74%
International affiliations:	UN, OAS, LAFTA, Group of 77
Defence expenditure:	$41m.

Paraguay was a Spanish Jesuit colony and became independent in 1811. The country lies in the centre of South America; to the south Argentina, to the north-west Bolivia and to the east Brazil. 50% of the country is scrub and marshland, the Chaco, west of the river Paraguay where 4% of the population lives. East of the river, animals graze and crops are grown in fertile grassland and large unexploited reserves of hardwood and cedars are found on rolling, hilly country. There are few minerals. Hydro-electricity is the booming activity. Paraguay already exports it to Argentina and Brazil. At Itaipa, the largest hydro-electric project in the world is due for completion in 1983. The capital, Asunción, with 400 000 inhabitants, is in the south where the River Paraguay meets the Argentine frontier.

Natural resources: Iron, manganese, copper, uranium
Crops: Cotton, tobacco, soybeans, wheat, maize, manioc, sweet potatoes, rice
Animals: Cattle, horses, pigs, sheep
Agriculture: 27% of land, 53% of work-force
Industry: Processing food, especially meat-packing, timber products, consumer goods, oil-refining, vegetable oils, cement
Exports: Beef, cotton, oil-seeds, timber, vegetable oils, tobacco, tea, hides
Imports: Vehicles, fuel, machinery, food, drink, tobacco, textiles, iron
Partners: Argentina, Brazil, USA, Germany, Netherlands, Algeria
Education: Free; supposedly compulsory but many areas lack

schools despite intense building programmes (1978). 8 000 students at university

Communications: 12 000 km of roads; navigation on Paraguay River, Concepción to Asunción (288 km) and thence 1520 km to the sea (Rio del la Plata)

Peru

Population:	17.4m.
GNP:	$12.4bn.
Growth rate per capita:	0.7%
Development assistance per capita:	$5.03
Literacy rate:	68%
International affiliations:	UN, OAS, ANCOM, LAFTA, Group of 77, N/A
Defence expenditure:	$366m.

Peru was the centre of Inca civilization and subsequently the Spanish empire and obtained independence in 1824 after four years of fighting. The country lies on the north-west coast of South America. Chile is to the south, Bolivia and Brazil to the east, Colombia to the north and Ecuador to the north-west. The dry, economically active coastal zone extends up to 160 km inland to the Andes mountains. The mountain zone reaches 6 600 m and spreads for 320 km to the humid, forested, eastern lowlands known as the Montana occupying about half of Peru but largely uninhabited. In the early 1970s the Velasco government introduced the Plan Inca designed to place the economy under collective and co-operative control, but they ran into problems of external debts, balance of payments deficit and inflation. The Bermuda government adopted a new, Tupac Amaru Plan in 1977 aiming at 'participatory socialist democracy' but designed not to discourage private investment. The capital, Lima, is in the centre of the coastline with a population of 4 million. There is high unemployment, up to 40% of the work-force.

Natural resources: Copper, lead, zinc, silver, iron, uranium, coal, salt, limestone
Crops: Maize, grains, sugar, cotton, coffee
Animals: Horses, cattle, goats, sheep, pigs, poultry, alpaca, vicuna
Agriculture: 23% of land, 43% of work-force, 13% of GDP

Industry: Mineral processing, fishmeal, oil-refining, textiles, light engineering
Exports: Copper, lead, silver, zinc, iron, fish products, oil, coffee, sugar, cotton, wool
Imports: Machinery, fuel, chemicals, food, iron, cereals, pharmaceuticals
Partners: USA, Germany, Japan, Ecuador, Venezuela, UK, Benelux
Education: Free and compulsory 7–16 but few schools; 105 000 students at 33 universities
Communications: 45 000 km of roads, 1 600 km of railways including the highest standard gauge railway in the world at 4500 m

Philippines

Population:	49m.
GNP:	$29bn.
Growth rate per capita:	3.6%
Development assistance per capita:	$4.18
Literacy rate:	83%
International affiliations:	UN, ADB, ASEAN, Colombo Plan, Group of 77
Defence expenditure:	$764m.

The Philippines were a Spanish colony from the sixteenth century, governed by the USA from 1898 and occupied by the Japanese in 1942. Full independence came in 1946. The country comprises a 1 100 km-long archipelago, south of Taiwan, north-east of Borneo, separating the South China Sea from the Pacific Ocean. In all there are 7 100 islands of which Luzon and Mindanao are the biggest and most densely populated. The capital Manila (pop. 4.5 million) is in Luzon. The climate is generally warm (80°F) and humid with up to 540 cm of rain. There are also frequent typhoons, active volcanoes and occasional earthquakes. The economy grew rapidly from 1945–55, more slowly until 1965 and then rapidly again until 1973. Growth in the late 1970s did not reach planned targets. However, government agricultural programmes (irrigation, fertilizer, seeds, pesticides, credit) achieved self-sufficiency in rice in 1976. Industrial production is shifting from import substitution to goods for export. Earlier problems with fluctuating world prices and lack of investment capital pushed the Philippines into the arms of the IMF in 1970. Growth has been generated largely by private investment supported by substantial government incentives and publicly-financed infrastructure.

Natural resources: Copper, iron, other minerals
Crops: Rice, maize, coconut oil, sugar, copra, hemp, tobacco
Animals: Water buffalo, cattle, goats, poultry
Forestry: The Philippines are one of the biggest exporters of logs, lumber and plywood but world demand has fallen.
Agriculture: 38% of land, 49% of work-force
Industry: Processed food, drink, tobacco, rubber, cement, glass, textiles, chemicals, fertilizer, iron and steel, refined oil; 25% of GDP
Exports: Coconut oil, copper, sugar, logs, copra, iron, lumber, bananas
Imports: Oil, transport equipment, metal, chemicals, electrical machinery, fuel, food
Partners: USA, Japan, Saudi Arabia, Kuwait, Netherlands, Australia, West Germany
Education: 9½ million pupils at 42 000 schools; 15% of budget; 27 000 students at University of the Philippines
Communications: 63 000 km of roads

Rwanda

Population:	4.5m.
GNP:	1bn.
Growth rate per capita:	1.0%
Development assistance per capita:	$19.32
Literacy rate:	25%
International affiliations:	UN, OAU, OCAM, Group of 77, N/A
Defence expenditure:	$19m.

Rwanda was administered by the UK as part of the UN Trust Territory of Ruanda Urundi until independence in 1962. The country lies within 5° south of the Equator in East Africa with Burundi to the south, Zaire to the west, Uganda north and Tanzania east. Families live in compounds not villages. There are a few towns left by the British including Kigali the capital (pop.60 000). The people live by subsistence agriculture. Overpopulation and irregular rainfall lead to famine.

Traditionally, Rwandan society is feudal with the Hutu (89% of the population) dominated by the Tutsi or Watusi (10%), although the present government is pledged to end feudalism. Short-term borrowing and large deficits led to IMF intervention in 1966. The government is trying to improve agriculture and foreign aid is devoted to developing electric power, improving communications, swamp drainage and increasing production, notably of tea.

Natural resources: Cassiterite, wolfram, methane (Lake Kiva)
Crops: Coffee, tea, pyrethrum, cassava, maize, (also rice project)
Animals: Ankole cattle (feudal status symbol, low value), goats, sheep
Agriculture: 95% of work-force, 39% of land
Industry: Food-processing, construction, minerals, light consumer goods; under 5% of work-force, 23% GDP
Exports: Coffee, tea, cassiterite, pyrethrum, wolfram
Imports: Textiles, food, machinery, oil products. Imports generally arrive by ship in Mombasa (Kenya), travel by rail to Kampala (Uganda) and by truck to Kigali.
Partners: Belgium and Luxembourg, Japan, Kenya, West Germany, France
Education: 37% primary attendance, 2% secondary; University at Butare
Communications: 18 400 km of road, shipping on Lake Kiva

Saudi Arabia

Population:	8.22m.
GNP:	$94.6bn.
Growth rate per capita:	11.8%
Development assistance per capita:	$0.83
Literacy rate:	30%
International affiliations:	UN, OPEC, OAPEC, Arab League, Group of 77, N/A
Defence expenditure:	$20.7bn.

Saudi Arabia was united in 1932 and occupies four-fifths of the Arabian peninsular. In the south of the peninsular are the two Yemens, in the south-east Oman, the United Arab Emirates and Qatar. The country is largely desert with 5–10cm of rain, summer temperatures above 120°F and winter sometimes below freezing. The area called the Hejaz, on the northern half of the Red Sea coast, is the commercial centre containing the towns of Medina, Jeddah and Mecca. The southern Red Sea coast is paralleled by the mountainous Asir region. The capital Riyadh (pop. 660 000) lies in the centre of the country in the Nejd where wheat and barley are grown. East of Riyadh, along the Persian Gulf is Hasa, the richest oil-bearing area in the world. The production of oil (discovered in the 1930s) is the basis of the economy. The government spends some of the oil revenue on diversification, industrialization, infrastructure and social services. Growth rates reached 16.3% in the early 1970s with 10.2% projected for 1980. Skilled manpower remains in short supply and over a million foreigners work in Saudi Arabia.

Natural resources: Oil, natural gas, iron, gold, copper, possibly uranium
Crops: Dates, wheat, maize, alfalfa, grapes, rice
Animals: Camels, horses, sheep, cattle, goats, asses (20% of population still nomadic)
Agriculture: 40% of land grazed, 1% cultivable; 75% of work-force
Industry: Oil-refining, fertilizer, cement; 10% of work-force
Exports: Oil and products (over 95% exports, over 90% government revenue)
Imports: Transport equipment, machinery, food
Partners: Japan, France, Italy, USA, Netherlands, UK
Education: Free. Girls' schools introduced in 1962. University of Riyadh
Communications: 570 km of metalled roads, railway, deep-water ports. Caravans still cross the desert.

Senegal

Population:	5.6m.
GNP:	$2.14bn.
Growth rate per capita:	-2.2%
Development assistance per capita:	$24.85
Literacy rate:	10%
International affiliations:	UN, OAU, OCAM, ACP, Group of 77, N/A
Defence expenditure:	(9 400 men)

Senegal obtained independence from France in 1959, firstly as part of the short-lived Mali Federation then separately in 1960. A country of low plains, savannah and rain-forest, the republic is in the middle of the West African coast with Mauritania to the north, Mali to the east, Guinea and Guinea Bissau south and the enclave of the Gambia along the banks of that river in southern Senegal. The country depends upon agriculture but harvests are subject to unreliable weather and have fallen while the population has grown. In particular, droughts from 1966 to 1972 were disastrous and more are expected. The fifth Development Plan (1977–81) devotes investment to mineral exploitation, tourism, cotton, fishing, livestock, seeds and rice. The government pursues socialism built upon African traditions but seeks to encourage foreign investment. Dakar, the capital (pop. 798 000), lies in the centre of the coastline with a large airport, important to transatlantic networks and a duty-free industrial zone.

Natural resources: Phosphates, iron ore
Crops: Groundnuts, maize, rice, cotton, millet, sorghum
Fishing: Commercial and growing; modern boats in use
Agriculture: 60% of land, 70% of work-force
Industry: Peanut oil, fertilizer, cement, processed food, canned fish, oil-refining – nearly all around Dakar. 8% of work-force
Exports: Groundnuts, phosphates, preserved fish
Imports: Rice, sugar, petroleum products, textiles, machinery
Partners: France, Netherlands, USA, Mauritania
Education: 40% attendance but resources already stretched. University at Dakar
Communications: Best road network in West Africa. Railway, Dakar to Bamako (Mali)

Sierra Leone

Population:	3.39m.
GNP:	$838m.
Growth rate per capita:	-1.5%
Development assistance per capita:	$6.08
Literacy rate:	10%
International affiliations:	UN, CW, OAU, ECOWAS, AFBD, ACP, Group of 77, N/A
Defence expenditure:	$11.3m.

Sierra Leone was a British colony until independence in 1961. The capital, Freetown (pop. 246 000) was established by freed slaves in 1787. The country lies on the south-west coast of West Africa between Liberia (south) and Guinea (north and east). The coastal area is swamp, the hinterland wooded and hilly and the east high plateau. The country lies between 7 and 10° north of the Equator; temperatures vary around 80°F and the rainfall reaches 500 cm on the coast. The economy is based upon agriculture and minerals, principally diamonds. Balance of payment problems and public borrowing led to calling in the IMF and the imposition of restrictions in 1977. The priority now is to improve agriculture and increase food production.

Natural resources: Diamonds, bauxite, rutile, chromite, iron ore
Crops: Coffee, cocoa, ginger, rice, piassava, cassava, maize, palm-kernels
Animals: Cattle, poultry, pigs
Agriculture: 30% of land, 75% of work-force, 30% of national income
Industry: Diamond, bauxite, rutile mining; drink, tobacco, construction, tourism, oil mills, timber, joinery, rice mills
Exports: Minerals (70%, 1975), coffee, cocoa, ginger
Imports: Food, drink, tobacco, raw materials, chemicals, machinery
Partners: UK, USA, Japan, West Germany, Netherlands, Nigeria
Education: Fourah Bay College (founded 1827) was the educational centre of British West Africa and is now part of the University of Sierra Leone. Education is neither free nor compulsory: 205 000 primary pupils, 48 000 secondary.
Communications: The road network is expanding: over 6400 km of main roads. Freetown is a natural harbour.

Singapore

Population:	2.4m.
GNP:	$8.1bn.
Growth rate per capita:	7.0%
Development assistance per capita:	$5.57
Literacy rate:	77%
International affiliations:	UN, ASEAN, CW, Colombo Plan, Group of 77

Defence expenditure: $1.26bn.

Singapore was a British possession from 1819, briefly joined the Federation of Malaysia in 1963 and became independent in 1965. The country consists of one large island and the 55 small ones off the tip of the Malay peninsula, separated from Malaysia by the Straits of Johore, with Indonesia as its neighbour across the sea to the west, south and east. Once jungle and swamp, Singapore is now almost entirely urban with a high population density. Half the people are under 21 and a third under 10. Two degrees north of the Equator, temperatures reach 87 F on average and rainfall 240 cm. Singapore has undergone rapid industrialization since the war, developing light and heavy industries. The government now favours capital-intensive, high-technology industries. Growth rates averaged 16%, 1965–70, and 14%, 1968–72. Singapore has become the commercial centre of South-East Asia deriving large incomes from entrepot trade, banking, shipping and insurance. The government ensures wage stability and a quiescent work-force and successfully attracts foreign investment through its Economic Development Board which has established industrial estates with financial incentives. 60% of housing is also government-owned.

Crops: Orchids, vegetables, fruit
Animals: Poultry, pigs
Agriculture: 2% of work-force, 1.1% GNP
Industry: Oil-refining and exploration, ship-repair, rubber-processing, electronics, coffee, timber, copra-processing, construction, tourism. Manufacturing 24.9% GNP, 27% of work-force (Trade increased 18%, 1976–7, and 15.3% 1977–8)
Partners: Malaysia, Japan, Saudi Arabia, USA, Hong Kong, UK
Education: Not compulsory, 66% attendance. Aim: 10 years for all. Centralized syllabus includes compulsory technical subjects. Two universities and two polytechnics
Communications: Over 2000 km metalled roads, railway to Malaysia; new airport at Changi, fourth-largest port in world (by tonnage)

Somalia (Somali Democratic Republic)

Population:	3.5m.
GNP:	$425m.
Growth rate per capita:	-0.8%
Development assistance per capita:	$23.87
Literacy rate:	20%
International affiliations:	UN, OAU, Arab League, ACP, Group of 77, N/A
Defence expenditure:	$95m.

Somalia was created in 1960 by the union of the former British and Italian Somalilands. The country forms a figure 7 on the coast of the Horn of Africa with the Gulf of Aden to the north and the Indian Ocean to the east. Kenya lies to the south-west, Ethiopia to the west and a short frontier with Djibouti in the north-west. Spreading 12° north from the Equator, Somalia is hot (65–105°F) and subject to monsoon winds and recurring drought. 60% of the people are nomadic pastoralists, and livestock form the main wealth of the country. Agriculture including modern plantations is concentrated around the rivers Juba and Uebi-Shibeli. Self-help projects led by youth volunteers have developed urban electrification, schools, paved roads. Priorities of the 1979–81 Development Plan are livestock, agriculture and minerals. The capital Mogadishu (pop. 400 000) is on the southern part of the coast, and the EEC and the World Bank have financed the construction of a deep-water port there.

Natural resources: Uranium – unexploited; oil exploration continues, gypsum reported.
Crops: Bananas, maize, sugar-cane, cassava, sorghum, beans, peanuts, cotton
Animals: Camels, sheep, goats
Agriculture: 13% of land is arable, 32% grazing; 60% of workforce
Industry: Textiles, meat, fish and fruit-juice processing, sugar-refining
Exports: Livestock, skins, hides, fresh fruit (notably bananas)
Imports: Machinery, manufactures, transport equipment
Partners: Saudi Arabia, Italy, USSR, Thailand, China
Education: Nomadic life-style inhibits progress. 2800 students at university. Mass literacy campaign in 1975

Communications: 14 400 km of road (1 120 km all-weather), trucks and buses most common transport. No railway

Sri Lanka

Population:	14.5m.
GNP:	$2.8bn.
Growth rate per capita:	2.0%
Development assistance per capita:	$10.83
Literacy rate:	85%
International affiliations:	UN, CW, ADB, Colombo Plan, Group of 77, N/A
Defence expenditure:	$26.5m.

Formerly the British colony of Ceylon, Sri Lanka became independent in 1972. The country is a pear-shaped island, 29 km off the south-east coast of India. Most of the land is low plain, but in the south-centre there are hills and mountains rising to 2 100 m. Sri Lanka lies between 7° and 9° north of the Equator with temperatures of 80°F most of the year and rainfall reaching 500 cm in the south. The British introduced tea, rubber and coconut plantations and Tamils from southern India to work on them. Half the population was Tamil when independence was granted and without rights in Sri Lanka or India but they have now received citizenship or have been repatriated. Agitation for Tamil independence continues in the north. In the 1950s and 1960s the government succeeded in reducing infant mortality, increasing literacy and redistributing resources toward the rural poor. The economy became unbalanced in the 1970s when export earnings ceased to finance increasingly expensive imports (including food and oil) needed by a growing population. Social services were cut and foreign aid increased, including a family planning programme. Much of the economy has been nationalized but foreign investment is encouraged by tax holidays. The capital Colombo (pop. 890 000) is on the east coast.

Natural resources: Limestone, graphite, minerals, precious and semi-precious stones
Crops: Tea, coconuts, rubber, rice, spices
Animals: Cattle, buffalo, goats, sheep, pigs, poultry
Agriculture: 39% of land is cultivated; 45% of work-force
Industry: Consumer goods, textiles, chemicals, light engineer-

ing, paper; oldest industry is salt production by evaporating seawater in sunlight.

Exports: Tea, rubber, coconut

Imports: Food, drink, oil, fertilizer, consumer goods, capital goods

Partners: Saudi Arabia, USA, Pakistan, Japan, Iran, China, UK

Education: Free from kindergarten to university. 16 000 students at university

Communication: 26 560 km of roads, 1 493 km of railway

Sudan

Population:	18.4m.
GNP:	$6.15bn.
Growth rate per capita:	0.5%
Development assistance per capita:	$8.08%
Literacy rate:	20%
International affiliations:	UN, Arab League, OAU, ACP, Group of 77, N/A
Defence expenditure:	$242m.

Sudan was conquered and unified by Egypt in 1821 and re-conquered by the UK and Egypt in 1898 after the Mahdi's revolt. Independence from the UK and Egypt came in 1954. It is the largest country in Africa, occupying the area from the Red Sea and Ethiopia in the east to Libya, Chad and the Central African Republic in the west; from Egypt to Zaire, Uganda and Kenya to the south. The capital Khartoum (pop. 250 000) lies in the heart of the country at the junction of the Blue Nile and the White Nile. Every kind of African terrain is found from tropical forest, savanna, swamp and scrub to sandy steppe and desert. Climate varies: in Khartoum, temperatures reach 100°F most of the year but humidity is low. From 1955–71 there was virtual civil war between the northern Arabic Muslims and the southerners who are subsistence farmers, animists in belief and speaking a number of different local languages. In 1972 autonomy for the south was agreed. Development has been very limited; transport is difficult and expensive and resources scarce. Nevertheless, investment in cotton production, supported by irrigation, has been successful.

Natural resources: Iron ore, copper, chrome in small amounts; gold; oil exploration
Crops: Sorghum, sugar-cane, peanuts, cotton, wheat, sesame, gum arabic
Animals: Cattle, sheep, goats, poultry, camels
Forestry: Gum arabic grown in the south is the second biggest cash-crop.
Agriculture: 20% of land is arable; 86% of work-force
Industry: Cement, textiles, pharmaceuticals, shoes, food-processing
Exports: Cotton (55%), peanuts, sesame, gum arabic, livestock
Imports: Fertilizer, machinery, sugar, cotton fabric, motor vehicles, food
Partners: UK, Italy, Japan, West Germany, USA
Education: 20% attendance for first four years; 7 000 students at university. Government grants for village schools
Communications: 4 000 km of railway; 1 440 km of surfaced roads; river steamers; Port Sudan seaport

Swaziland

Population:	0.5m.
GNP:	$320m.
Growth rate per capita:	4.9%
Development assistance per capita:	$40.40
Literacy rate:	36%
International affiliations:	UN, OAU, CW, South African Customs Union, N/A
Defence expenditure:	n/a

Swaziland came under British rule in 1903 and gained independence in 1968. King Sobhuza II has been on the throne since 1901 (under his mother's regency until 1921). The country is almost completely surrounded by the Transvaal province of South Africa. The eastern border is with Mozambique and Natal (another South African province). The land descends from the western highveld through the middleveld to the lowveld and the Lubombo Plateau in the east. The climate is generally subtropical and dry, depending upon altitude: temperatures up to 72°F and rainfall up to 112cm. Most of the population is engaged in rearing livestock or growing subsistence crops. 29 000 people work abroad, mainly in South Africa. Given its limited resources, Swaziland is prosperous but much of the wealth is in the hands of foreign investors and landowners. The capital Mbabane has a population of 22 000.

Natural resources: Iron ore (no longer mined), asbestos, coal
Crops: Maize, sugar-cane, citrus, cotton, rice, pineapples
Animals: Cattle, goats, sheep, poultry
Agriculture: 8% of land arable; 85% of work-force
Industry: Sugar-mills, cotton-mills, meat processing, pulp mills, tourism, chemicals, machinery, drinks, consumer goods. Generally small-scale industry, local entrepreneurs
Exports: Sugar, wood products, asbestos, citrus fruit, beef, hides, skins
Imports: Motor vehicles, fuel, oil, food, clothing
Partners: South Africa, UK, USA, Japan
Education: 92 700 primary pupils, 17 400 secondary (1976) – generally church and mission schools. University of Botswana and Swaziland
Communications: Railway to Maputo (Mozambique). Daily buses between towns. 241 km of tarred roads

Syria

Population:	8.8m.
GNP:	$9.2bn.
Growth rate per capita:	4.7%
Development assistance per capita:	$8.20
Literacy rate:	41%
International affiliations:	UN, Arab League, Group of 77, N/A
Defence expenditure:	$4.4bn.

The area which now forms Syria was part of the Ottoman Empire and became an independent Arab Kingdom in 1920. The League of Nations created a French mandate and Syria finally became independent in 1946. The republic lies on the east coast of the Mediterranean, south of Turkey, west of Iraq and north of Jordan. Between southern Syria and the sea lie the Lebanon and Israel. The climate is dry and hot in the summer and cold in the winter. The capital Damascus (pop. 2 million) lies in one of the valley oases east of the anti-Lebanon mountains which follow the coastline. It is one of the oldest cities in the world (founded *c.* 2500 BC). Development programmes have been ambitious, supported by oil revenues and Arab grants and loans. The Euphrates river, running from north to south-east, a traditional basin of cultivation, has been dammed to provide power and irrigation. Military expenditure exceeds half of the total budget. Continued oil production depends upon new finds. Oil from Iraq and Saudi Arabia is piped through Syria to the Mediterranean. Syria has to pay world prices to provide sufficient crude for its refineries.

Natural resources: Chrome and manganese, asphalt, iron, salt, phosphate, oil, natural gas
Crops: Cotton, wheat, barley, tobacco, sugar-beet, grapes, tomatoes
Animals: Cattle, sheep, goats, poultry
Agriculture: 65% of land, 51% of work-force; 16% GDP (1975)
Industry: Textiles, fertilizer, cement, glass, oil refining, food-processing, soap, phosphates, tourism. 15% of work-force, 20.3% GDP (1974)
Exports: Cotton, fruit, vegetables, oil, wood, tobacco, textiles, phosphates, cereals, livestock, hides and skins
Imports: Food, fuel, machinery, transport equipment, textiles, metals, chemicals, fertilizer
Partners: West Germany, Italy, Japan, France, USA, USSR
Education: Free and compulsory 6–11. Three universities
Communications: 8 000 km surfaced roads; Damascus–Baghdad pullman coach; ports of Tatus and Latakiya growing

Taiwan (Republic of China)

Population:	18m.
GNP:	$32.3bn.
Growth rate per capita:	6.6%
Development assistance per capita:	n/a
Literacy rate:	n/a
International affiliations:	World Bank, IMF, ADB
Defence expenditure:	$1.75bn.

Taiwan is the large island off the south-east coast of mainland China, where Chiang Kai-shek and the nationalist Chinese retreated in 1949. The Republic is situated between the East and South China seas and includes the Quemoy and Matsu islands within 8 km of the mainland coast. A mountain range runs from north to south down the eastern side of Taiwan. The climate is semi-tropical, very hot and wet in the summer; there are earthquakes, typhoons and floods. The 1960s and 1970s witnessed the rapid transformation from a predominantly agricultural economy to an industrial one. Export-led growth and private investment characterized the development of labour-intensive light industry producing textiles, electronics and electrical machinery, plastics, toys and sporting goods. The volume of trade tripled every five years from 1955 to 1975. Since 1973 Taiwan has been adversely affected by world recession and inflation. To stabilize the economy, the emphasis has shifted to developing heavy industry and infrastructure. As a result, steel, pig-iron, aluminium and cement production has grown, along with shipbuilding. There was one nuclear power station in operation and two under construction in 1977. Taiwanese agriculture is very intensive, producing two to three crops annually but only a quarter of land is cultivable. The Republic is self-sufficient in paddy rice and exports pork, but has to import food, especially grain. Two-thirds of imports are food and raw materials. There is a large fishing fleet and much of the catch is exported. Main trading partners are the USA, Japan, Hong Kong and Germany. Education is free and compulsory from 6 to 15. There are 8 universities. 45% of the population is under 20 and 27% are still at school. There are excellent roads and railways.

Tanzania

Population:	17.5m.
GNP:	$3.9bn.
Growth rate per capita:	2.1%
Development assistance per capita:	n/a
Literacy rate:	50%
International affiliations:	UN, OAU, CW, ACP, Group of 77, N/A
Defence expenditure:	$303m.

Tanzania was formed in 1964 by the union of Tanganyika and Zanzibar. Tanganyika had been a German colony, mandated to the UK by the League of Nations and independent since 1962. Zanzibar was an Arab possession until 1890 when the UK took over, and became independent in 1963. Tanzania consists now of the islands of Pemba and Zanzibar and the mainland from Uganda and Kenya in the north to Zambia, Malawi and Mozambique in the south; from Rwanda, Burundi and Zaire in the west to the Indian Ocean. Most of the country is within 10° south of the Equator and the climate is hot except in the highlands and the lake areas; the coastal plains are humid and the central plateau dry. Half of Lakes Victoria and Tanganyika and a quarter of Lake Nyasa are within Tanzania's frontiers, yet two-thirds of the country is unsuitable for cultivation because of insufficient water and tsetse-fly. The capital Dar es Salaam (pop. 500 000) is in the centre of the coastline. The principles of Tanzanian development were laid down in the Arusha Declaration of 1967. The basic concept is *ujamaa* (familyhood), improving rural living standards without dependence on foreign aid but through egalitarian co-operatives and public ownership. Zanzibar's economy is based upon the export of cloves (mainly to Indonesia) grown on Pemba. Tanzania has suffered balance of payments difficulties and the third 5-year Plan (1977–82) emphasizes support for basic industry to produce cheap goods for home consumption and to save foreign exchange.

Natural resources: Iron and coal, diamonds, gold, off-shore gas
Crops: Sugar, sisal, maize, rice, wheat, cotton, coffee, cashew, nuts, tea, tobacco, pyrethrum, cloves
Animals: Cattle, sheep, goats, poultry
Agriculture: 15% of land, 90% of work-force, 75% of exports
Industry: Textiles, agricultural processing, tyres, fertilizer, steel, oil-refining, cement
Exports: Coffee, cotton, petroleum products, cloves, sisal, diamonds, coconuts, hides and skins, timber, beeswax
Imports: Manufactures, textiles, machinery, transport equipment, food, tobacco
Education: 100% attendance decreed (1977); 95 300 primary pupils, 8 000 secondary (1976); University of Dar es Salaam
Communications: 6 400 km improved roads; 2 560 km railway plus the 1 840 km long Tanzam railway to Zambia built by Chinese engineers

Thailand

Population:	47.8m.
GNP:	$21.9bn.
Growth rate per capita:	4.4%
Development assistance per capita:	$2.18

Literacy rate:	82%
International affiliations:	UN, ADB, ASEAN, Colombo Plan, Group of 77, N/A
Defence expenditure:	$1.09bn.

Thai civilization goes back to the fifth millennium BC. The government was modernized by King Rama V (upon whom *The King and I* was based) in the late nineteenth century and the country escaped colonization. Thailand occupies the central portion of South-East Asia with Burma to the west and Laos and Cambodia to the east. The southern part of the country extends down the Malay peninsular to Malaysia and frames the Gulf of Thailand. The central area is well irrigated and agriculturally rich; the north-east suffers from floods and droughts; the west is forested mountain country and the south is rainforest. The capital Bangkok (pop.4.5million) lies 30 km up the River Chao Phya on the Gulf of Thailand. There was a slump in 1974–6 and the fourth Five-Year Plan (1977–82) aims to revive the economy, decrease the disparity between town and country, diversify agriculture and increase production. Balance of payments problems have been aggravated by drought, but Thailand has good reserves of foreign exchange and a low debt-service ratio which enables the country to borrow further money easily. Projects are under way to develop hydro-electricity, irrigation, railways, ports, highways and education.

Natural resources: Natural gas (in the Gulf), flourite, tin, tungsten, manganese, iron, antimony
Crops: Rice, rubber, maize, tapioca, sugar
Animals: Elephants, horses, buffalo, cattle, pigs, poultry
Forestry: 60% land. Teak is harvested using elephants and floated down river to Bangkok
Agriculture: 34% land arable, 76% of work-force
Industry: Food-processing, textiles, wood and paper, cement, sugar, tobacco, food. Nuclear reactor since 1961 and more under construction
Exports: Rice, tin, tapioca, sugar, rubber, maize, pineapple, textiles, teak, jute
Imports: Transport and construction equipment, machinery, crude oil, fibres, chemicals, manufactures, tobacco
Partners: Japan, USA, Netherlands, Saudi Arabia, Qatar, Singapore, West Germany

Education: Free and compulsory 7–14; 12 universities
Communications: 3 700 km of railway, highways to large towns

Togo

Population:	2.6m.
GNP:	$768m.
Growth rate per capita:	5.6%
Development assistance per capita:	$21.45
Literacy rate:	10%
International affiliations:	UN, OAU, ACAM, ECOWAS, ACP, Group of 77, N/A
Defence expediture:	$27.8m.

Togo is a north-south strip of land on the south coast of West Africa between Ghana (to the west) and Dahomey (to the east). Its northern frontier is with Upper Volta. Formerly French Togoland, it was once part of the German colony of Togo (the other part, British Togoland, joined Ghana) and became independent in 1960. The country lies within 10° north of the Equator and is generally hot and humid, temperatures exceeding 100°F in the north. Most Togolese do not participate in the cash economy and depend on subsistence agriculture. The government has developed the cultivation of coffee and cocoa for export. Phosphates are the key to Togo's finances since nationalization in 1974. Budgets are generally balanced, the debt-service ratio is 21% and there is investment in building, roads, ports, tourism and education. The capital Lomé (pop. 130 000) is the major port and industrial centre; there is an oil refinery and the Lomé Convention regulating trade and aid between the European Community and ACP countries was signed there.

Natural resources: Phosphates, limestone, iron; oil and uranium exploitation
Crops: Cocoa, coffee, maize, cassava, groundnuts, yams, manioc, millet, sorghum
Animals: Cattle, sheep, pigs, horses, asses, goats
Industry: Phosphate processing, textiles, agricultural processing, oil refinery, cement works
Exports: Phosphates (53%), cocoa (17%), coffee (16%)
Imports: Consumer goods, fuels, machinery, cotton fabrics,

transport equipment, food
Partners: France, Netherlands, West Germany, UK, Japan
Education: 50% attendance 5–19; University of Benin – 2 200 students
Communications: 1 100 km paved road, 443 km railway

Trinidad and Tobago

Population:	1.03m.
GNP:	$3 420
Growth rate per capita:	2.7%
Development assistance per capita:	$4.77
Literacy rate:	78%
International affiliations:	UN, Caricom, CW, OAS, ACP, Group of 77, N/A
Defence expenditure:	n/a

Trinidad was visited by Columbus in 1498, passed to the UK in 1797, merged with Tobago in 1888, formed part of the West Indies Federation in 1958 and became independent in 1962. The two islands of Trinidad and Tobago are the southernmost in the Lesser Antilles chain in the West Indies. Trinidad, 11km off the coast of Venezuela, has three mountain ranges and is 50% forest; there are coastal swamps and the biggest asphalt bog in the world, in the south-west. Tobago, much smaller, north-east of Trinidad, has small-scale farming, tourist beaches and the town of Scarborough. The capital and commercial centre is Port-of-Spain (pop. 250 000). The economy depends upon the export of sugar and oil. Attempts to introduce dairy-farming failed in the 1920s and 1930s but a beef industry has now developed. Infrastructure is good and manufacturing industry is growing.

Natural resources: Oil, exploration continues
Crops: Sugar-cane, cocoa, coffee, rice, bananas, coconuts, citrus
Animals: Cattle, sheep, goats, pigs, poultry
Agriculture: 30% of land, 13% of work-force
Industry: Oil-refining, food-processing, cement, tourism
Exports: Petroleum products, chemicals, sugar
Imports: Crude oil, food, machinery, manufactures
Partners: USA, Saudi Arabia, Indonesia, UK, Iran, Guyana
Education: Free since 1960. 258 000 pupils, primary and

secondary (1973)
Communications: 4 208 km of road

Tunisia

Population:	6.4m.
GNP:	$6.99bn.
Growth rate per capita:	6.6%
Development assistance per capita:	$30.44
Literacy rate:	55%
International affiliations:	UN, Arab League, Group of 77, N/A
Defence expenditure:	$114m.

The territory now called Tunisia has been ruled by Phoenicians, Romans, Vandals, Greeks, Arabs, Turks and finally by France until independence in 1956. The country lies on the north coast of Africa, 144 km from Sicily. Algeria is to the west, Libya to the south-east. The Mediterranean Sea washes the north and east coasts. After independence most of the European managerial class left, foreign-owned land was nationalized and agriculture collectivized. The population grew fast and unemployment kept pace. Since 1969, Tunisia has benefited from increased world prices for phosphates and oil. Tourism has grown and investment in labour-intensive export-oriented industries has been attracted. Crops were damaged by drought in 1977 and unemployment remains high. The capital Tunis (pop. 1 million) in the north-east is the commercial centre with industry concentrated around it.

Natural resources: Oil, gas, phosphates, iron, lead, zinc
Crops: Wheat, olives, citrus, grapes
Animals: Horses, asses, mules, cattle, sheep, goats, camels, pigs
Fishery: Tunny, sponges (second-highest production in Mediterranean)
Agriculture: 45% of work-force, 19% GNP
Industry: Oil-refining, phosphates, olive oil, textiles, sugar-refining, cellulose plant, steel, fertilizer
Exports: Iron, phosphates, oil
Imports: Machinery, wheat, textiles, vehicles, pharmaceuticals, sugar and vegetable oil

Partners: France, Italy, West Germany, USA, Greece, Saudi Arabia

Education: Compulsory for 8 years; over 85% attendance; 33% national budget; free from primary to university

Communications: 16 600 km roads, 2 300 km railway

Uganda

Population:	12.5m.
GNP:	$8.36bn.
Growth rate per capita:	n/a
Development assistance per capita:	$1.57
Literacy rate:	n/a
International affiliations:	UN, CW, OAU, ACP, Group of 77, N/A
Defence expenditure:	(7 000 men)

Uganda became independent from the UK in 1962. From 1971 to 1979 under the rule of Idi Amin, the economy deteriorated and the government of Milton Obote, returned in controversial elections in 1980, faces the task of reconstruction. The country is landlocked in East Africa between Zaire in the west and Kenya in the east, Sudan in the north and Rwanda and Tanzania in the south. The Equator passes through Lake Victoria just south of Kampala, the capital. Uganda is hot and dry with less than 50cm rainfall in the north-east. Growth rates were generally negative throughout the 1970s although the non-monetary economy, i.e. barter, grew considerably. In 1977 a three-year Economic Action programme was launched but the objectives of renewing industry and increasing agricultural production were not met.

Natural resources: Copper, other metals

Crops: Coffee, tea, cotton, sugar, tobacco, oilseeds, groundnuts

Animals: Cattle, sheep, goats, pigs, poultry

Fishery: Fish-farming expanding in Lake Victoria

Agriculture: 30% of land, 90% of work-force, over half GDP, 90% exports

Industry: Agricultural processing, copper, cement, shoes, fertilizer, steel, drinks, hydro-electric scheme at Owen Falls

Exports: Coffee, cotton, tea, copper

Imports: Petroleum products, machinery, transport

equipment, food
Partners: USA, UK, Japan, Italy, France, Germany
Education: Secondary education includes technical subjects;
Makerere University
Communications: 2 240 km paved road, vital railway to Mombasa (Kenya)

Upper Volta

Population:	6.7m.
GNP per capita:	$745m.
Growth rate per capita:	2.2%
Development assistance per capita:	$14.93
Literacy rate:	10%
International affiliations:	UN, OAU, OCAM, ECOWAS, ACP, Group of 77, N/A
Defence expenditure:	$33m.

Upper Volta under French rule was part of the French West
African Federation and obtained independence in 1960. The
country lies landlocked in West Africa, north of the Ivory
Coast, Ghana, Togo and Dahomey. To the north are Mali and
Niger. Between 10° and 15° north of the Equator, Upper Volta
consists of savanna and low hills, hot and dry with desert winds
and rainfall less than 25cm in the north. The capital
Ouagadougou (pop. 172 000) is in the centre of the country.
The population is concentrated in the south and many migrate
to the Ivory Coast and Ghana for work. Soil erosion is reducing the potential of this country which may already be regarded as the poorest in Africa. The Second Development Plan
(1972–6) sought to achieve 4% annual growth but failed. The
third plan finishes in 1981.

Natural resources: Manganese, limestone, bauxite, gold,
copper, tin, graphite
Crops: Sorghum, millet, cowpeas, rice, maize, yams, cassava –
for food. Sesame, groundnuts, cotton, sisal, karite – for cash
Animals: Cattle, sheep, goats, horses, donkeys, (drought has
reduced numbers)
Agriculture: 70% of land, 95% of work-force
Industry: Processing food, textiles, metal, sisal twine
Exports: Livestock, cotton

Imports: Manufactures, machinery, food
Partners: France, Ivory Coast, USA, West Germany, UK, Italy
Education: 170 000 primary pupils, 19 000 secondary, 345 university students (1977)
Communications: 16 000 km of roads (one-quarter usable all year); railway – Ouagadougou to port of Abidjan (Ivory Coast)

Uruguay

Population:	3.3m.
GNP:	$3.7bn.
Growth rate per capita:	1.4%
Development assistance per capita:	$3.71
Literacy rate:	91%
International affiliations:	UN, OAS, LAFTA, Group of 77
Defence expediture:	$72m.

Uruguay became independent from Spain in 1828. The country is on the east coast of South America, with its southern coast on the Rio de la Plata. Brazil is to the north and Argentina west across the River Uruguay. The social and economic development of Uruguay accelerated in the early years of the twentieth century but has been relatively stagnant since the second world war. Stock-raising is the basic activity; there are fewer large landlords than in other South American countries. In 1978, the government launched a Programme of Economic Reform to stimulate and diversify exports, to lower protective tariffs and inflation and to increase public efficiency. Hydro-electricity is in use and new projects are under development. The capital Montevideo (pop. 1.5 million) is the main port and industrial centre and lies on the south coast.

Crops: Grains, rice, sugarbeet
Animals: 9 million cattle, 19 million sheep; horses, pigs, goats, poultry
Agriculture: 85% of land (94% of which for stock-raising), 11% of work-force (minimum agricultural wage by law)
Industry: Meat-processing, wool, hides, textiles, shoes and leather goods, cement, oil-refining, sugar-refining
Exports: Meat, wool, textiles, hides, shoes, leather goods, furs, fish

Imports: Fuel, chemicals, machinery, metal

Partners: Brazil, USA, West Germany, Argentina, Kuwait, Iraq

Education: Free and compulsory primary education; rest free; 16 000 students at University of the Republic, at Montevideo (founded 1849)

Communications: 5 000 km paved roads, four main railways; river transport

Venezuela

Population:	15.4m.
GNP:	$39.3bn.
Growth rate per capita:	3.0%
Development assistance per capita:	$0.47
Literacy rate:	80%
International affiliations:	UN, OAS, LAFTA, Andean Pact, Rio Pact, OPEC, Group of 77
Defence expenditure:	$804m.

Venezuela, led by Simon Bolivar, became independent from Spain in 1821 as part of Greater Colombia which split up in 1830. The country is on the north coast of South America with Colombia to the west, Brazil to the south and Guyana to the east. Most of the population is concentrated in the Andes in the north-west and along the coast where Caracas (pop.2.4million) the capital is situated. The *Ucenos* plains run south to the river Orinoco. Half of Venezuela lies south of this river, consisting largely of the Guiana highlands and occupied by only 4% of the population. At present growth rates the population will double in 20 years; more than half are under 15. Oil revenues are of great importance but other industries are developing. The government seeks to improve agriculture by provision of credit and irrigation, to stimulate industry by new technology and training, to transfer resources to the poorest third of the population and to correct the imbalance between urban growth and rural neglect. The country has very high gold and foreign reserves and is investing in hydro-electricity, communications and heavy industry in the un-developed Guiana region.

Natural resources: Oil (over 30% GNP and enough to continue

until next century), gas, iron, gold, diamonds, manganese, phosphates, sulphur
Crops: Rice, coffee, maize, cacao, sugar, bananas, beans
Animals: Over 10 million cattle, pigs, goats, sheep
Agriculture: 2% of land is cultivated; 20% work-force, 6% GNP
Industry: Oil-refining, iron and steel, paper, aluminium, textiles, transport equipment, consumer goods
Exports: Oil (over 90% foreign exchange earnings) iron, coffee, cocoa
Imports: Machinery, transport equipment, manufactures, chemicals, food
Partners: USA, Netherlands Antilles, Canada, UK, West Germany, Japan
Education: Free and compulsory 7–11, 60% primary attendance, 48% secondary. 15 universities with 225 000 students (1976)
Communications: 43 000 km all-weather roads; 3 700 km railway network construction started 1976

Vietnam

Population:	60m.
GNP:	$8.5bn.
Growth rate per capita:	n/a
Development assistance per capita:	n/a
Literacy rate:	n/a
International affiliations:	Comecon, UN, Group of 77
Defence expenditure:	(1m. men)

Vietnam was conquered by the French in 1884 and the Japanese in 1941 and was fought over between 1946 and 1975 when it was unified by the victory of North Vietnam. The country follows the east coast of South East Asia in the shape of a letter 'J'. China is to the north and Laos and Cambodia to the west. The terrain varies from the marshy deltas of the Mekong River in the south to the jungle highlands of the north. The climate is typical monsoon. In 1975 the task of reconstruction began with the northern economy based upon the centralized heavy industry badly damaged by bombing and the southern market economy destroyed. Southern industry depended heavily upon imported technology and raw materials and the war had distorted the distribution of resources: in 1970 service industries formed 70% GNP, employing the peasants who fled from the land and swelled the population of Saigon to 40% of the total. In 1978 all private trade was banned but the government has failed to replace the old private distribution network so insufficient food reaches the towns. Millions of Chinese have fled, leaving large gaps in the commercial and industrial structure. The 1976–80 Five-Year Plan was based upon the establishment of co-ordinated 'agro-industrial units' in new economic zones, designed to shift the peasants back to the countryside, to rebuild agriculture as a basis for light industry which in turn would be a base for heavy industry. Continued fighting, bad weather and resistance dragged the plan two years behind schedule. Foreign exchange and food imports are necessary. The capital, Hanoi (pop.2million), lies on the Red River in the north and Ho-Chi Minh City (formerly Saigon) (pop.3.4million) is far in the south.

Natural resources: Coal, oil and natural gas, iron, magnesium, titanium, bauxite
Crops: Rice, rubber, fruit, vegetables, maize, manioc, sugarcane
Animals: Cattle, pigs, goats, poultry
Forestry: Half of North Vietnam is forest, 300 million trees were planted in 1976–77 to replace those destroyed in the war.
Industry: Mining, food-processing, textiles, machine-building, cement, cotton, silk, handicrafts, 1979 industry working at 60% capacity
Exports: Agricultural products, coal, minerals
Imports: Technical equipment, raw materials, food, oil, medicine, fertilizer
Partners: USSR, Japan, Hong Kong, Singapore
Education: 13 million pupils (1978); state control; anti-illiteracy campaign and 'adult re-education programme'
Communication: 30 000 km of roads; Hanoi–Ho-Chi Minh City railway re-opened 1977; 4 800 km of navigable waterway

Yemen (North), Arab Republic of

Population:	5.3m.
GNP:	$1.5bn.
Growth rate per capita:	n/a
Development assistance per capita:	$9.1

Literacy rate:	22% male, 0.05% female
International affiliations:	UN, Arab League
Defence expenditure:	$79m.

North Yemen lies on the Red Sea in the south-west corner of Arabia, north of the Democratic Republic of Yemen and south of Saudi Arabia. The eastern boundary, also with Saudi Arabia, is undefined. The Tehama, a hot strip of semi-desert, runs down from Mecca into North Yemen along the Red Sea coast. The capital, Sana (pop. 130 000), is an ancient walled city in the mountains in the hinterland. There is a wide variety of crops but civil war (1965–66, republican against royalist) and drought decimated agricultural production. The 1976–81 Development Plan gives priority to infrastructure.

Natural resources: Copper, sulphur, coal, quartz, salt, but no oil
Crops: Wheat, sorghum, millet, coffee, gat (a narcotic), cotton, fruit
Animals: Cattle, camels, sheep, goats
Agriculture: 42% of land, 73% of work-force
Industry: Consumer goods, construction, weaving-mill, cement; oil-refinery planned
Exports: Cotton, coffee, hides and skins
Imports: Food, animals, machinery, transport equipment, textiles, sugar, fuel, chemicals
Partners: China, South Yemen, Italy, Saudi Arabia, West Germany, Japan
Education: 248 000 pupils including 3 000 students at Sana University (1977)
Communication: 1 650 km of roads

Yemen (South), People's Democratic Republic of

Population:	2.1m.
GNP:	$500m.
Growth rate per capita:	n/a
Development assistance per capita:	$14.68
Literacy rate:	20%
International affiliations:	UN, Arab League
Defence expenditure:	$56m.

Yemen, at the south-west corner of the Arabian peninsular,

consists of a flat, sandy coastal region from Aden to Al
Ghaydah, a mountainous hinterland and the islands of
Socotra in the Arabian Sea and Perim at the mouth of the
Red Sea. The country is dry (less than 7cm rainfall) and very
hot (up to 130°F in summer). The people are mainly engaged
in growing subsistence crops and herding. After the second
world war, cash crops were introduced, notably cotton which
became the main export, but production has now declined.
Cultivation is limited to fertile valleys and flood-plains;
traditional irrigation is being replaced by modern equipment.
There is virtually no industry beyond small-scale production
of consumer goods. The pre-independence economy was
based on the city of Aden as a bunkering station, entrepot
port and British military base. Following the Arab–Israeli
war in 1967 the Suez Canal was closed for many years. Trade
dropped enormously. The World Bank is supporting improvements to the Port of Aden. The BP refinery at Little
Aden provides the main source of government revenue, but
public salaries and civil service establishments have been cut.
Nationalization and seizures of workplaces by workers have
discouraged foreign investment.

Crops: Sorghum, sesame, millet, gat, cotton
Animals: Cattle, sheep, goats
Exports: Fish, gat, cotton
Education: 237 000 pupils in full-time education
Communication: 1 840 km of road, mostly unsurfaced

Zaire

Population:	28.2m.
GNP:	$2.3bn.
Growth rate per capita:	2.0%
Development assistance per capita:	$8.40
Literacy rate:	20%
International affiliations:	UN, OAU, ACP, Group of 77, N/A
Defence expenditure:	$50.5m.

Zaire, the former Belgian Congo, independent since 1960, is in
the centre of Africa. The Republic of Congo is the western
neighbour and Zaire has a corridor to the Atlantic Ocean on
the banks of the River Congo. Angola and Zambia lie to the

south, Tanzania, Burundi, Ruanda and Uganda to the east and
Sudan and the Central African Republic to the north. At independence the economy was relatively highly developed but
after seven years of fighting and disorder (1960–67) the
infrastructure was more or less destroyed. IMF intervention,
economic reform and rising copper prices then produced high
growth rates but these were followed by inflation and high
borrowing. The IMF stepped in again in 1976. Zaire has considerable mineral wealth, including oil in production since
1975. Agriculture remains the basis of the economy, with 85%
of the population in the countryside, mostly practising
traditional methods on small plots. The capital, Kinshasa
(pop. 1.8 million) (formerly Leopoldville), is an industrial
centre and lies in the south-west on the River Congo.

Natural resources: Copper, oil, cobalt, zinc, diamonds, manganese, tin, gold, bauxite, iron, coal
Crops: Coffee, palm oil, rubber, tea, cotton, cocoa – for cash;
manioc, bananas, maize, rice, vegetables, fruit, sugar – for
food
Animals: Cattle, sheep, goats, pigs, poultry
Industry: Mineral-processing, consumer goods, chemicals,
construction, steel
Exports: Copper, cobalt, diamonds, gold, manganese, coffee,
palm oil
Imports: Crude oil, petroleum products, chemicals, transport
equipment, textiles, food
Partners: USA, West Germany, Japan, Belgium, Luxem-
bourg, UK, France, Italy
Education: 85% attendance 6–11, 10% secondary, 1% tertiary
Communications: 150 000 km of earth-surfaced roads, 5 170 km
of railways

Zambia

Population:	5.7m.
GNP:	$2.54bn.
Growth rate per capita:	1.4%
Development assistance per capita:	$16.30
Literacy rate:	20%
International affiliations:	UN, OAU, CW, ACP, Group of 77, N/A
Defence expenditure:	$387m.

Zambia was formerly the British colony of Northern Rhodesia until independence in 1964. The country is landlocked in south central Africa with Botswana and Zimbabwe to the south, Mozambique and Malawi to the east, Tanzania and Zaire to the north and Angola to the west. The climate is subtropical with temperatures ranging from 48–90°F. Most of the people are subsistence farmers but the economy depends upon copper. Zambia is the world's largest exporter of copper. Development plans have concentrated on rural areas and self-sufficiency. Growth has been inhibited by a drop in the world price of copper in 1974 and the contemporaneous increase in oil prices. In addition to the resulting inflationary pressures, the government was one of the front-line states in the guerrilla war against the white régime in Rhodesia. In 1973, the Rhodesian border was closed and trade re-routed through Angola (until the railway was put out of action in 1975) and Tanzania (for the Tanzam Railway, see Tanzania). With a friendly government in Zimbabwe, conditions may improve but world demand remains low and imported oil remains expensive. The capital, Lusaka (pop. 415 000), is in the south-east.

Natural resources: Copper, zinc, lead, cobalt, coal
Crops: Maize, tobacco, cotton, groundnuts, sugar cane
Animals: Cattle, pigs, sheep, goats, poultry
Agriculture: 85% of work-force, 30% of land, 10% of GDP
Industry: Food-processing, chemicals, textiles, fertilizer; thermal and hydro-electricity (Kariba dam); virtually self-sufficient in energy
Exports: Copper, zinc, lead, cobalt, tobacco
Imports: Manufactures, electrical goods, fuel, machinery, transport equipment, chemicals, food
Partners: UK, USA, West Germany, Japan, Italy, Saudi Arabia, South Africa
Communications: Pre-independence transport links to South Africa, now to Tanzania and Malawi. More than 4 600 km of tarred roads. Railways to Zimbabwe, Zaire and Tanzania

Zimbabwe

Population:	7.3m.
GNP:	$3.3bn.
Growth rate per capita:	0.8%
Development assistance per capita:	n/a

Literacy rate:	30% (African), 100% (European)
International affiliations:	UN, OAU, Group of 77, CW, ACP, N/A
Defence expenditure:	$400m.

Zimbabwe became independent in April 1980, after 15 years of rebellion and guerrilla warfare following UDI. The country was formerly known as Rhodesia, officially Southern Rhodesia. Zimbabwe is landlocked in south-east Africa, separated from the Indian Ocean by Mozambique. Zambia is north across the River Zambia, Botswana to the west and South Africa to the south. The climate is subtropical. Agriculture is well-developed although much land lies abandoned while the government awaits funds to buy it from absentee white landowners. Industry was forced to diversify by UN sanctions against trade. Because of sanctions, trading figures are unavailable as most of it was clandestine. It is clear, however, that trade grew, the economy boomed in the early 1970s and is booming again now in 1981. In one year of reconstruction, the new government has resettled a million refugees, repaired roads, rebuilt bridges and opened up areas of the country virtually isolated under military or guerrilla control in recent years. Large sums of foreign aid are expected soon. 2000 whites have been leaving every month, reducing the available skilled manpower but the country still attracts skilled workers from abroad. The capital, Salisbury, is in the north-east.

Natural resources: Chrome, coal, asbestos, copper, nickel, gold, iron
Crops: Tobacco, maize, sorghum, wheat, sugar, cotton, tea, citrus
Animals: Cattle, asses, pigs, sheep, goats
Industry: Transport equipment, steel, metals, textiles, food-processing. Power network excellent, especially hydro-electricity from Kariba dam
Exports: No figures, but high potential in: tobacco, livestock, asbestos, copper, clothing, meat, chrome-ore, sugar, pig-iron, coal
Imports: No information, but capital and consumer goods and fuel needed
Partners: (potential) UK, rest of EEC, USA, South Africa, neighbouring African countries

Education: One million pupils in free, elementary education since independence; University of Zimbabwe

Communications: 10 000 km of paved main roads; railways to South Africa, Mozambique and Zambia

Further Reading

Books

Lars Anell and Birgitta Nygren, *The Developing Countries and the World Economic Order* (Frances Pinter Ltd, London, 1980)

Vincent Cable, *British Interests and Third World Development* (ODI, London, 1980)

Gary Field, *Poverty, Inequality and Development* (Cambridge University Press, 1980)

Andre Gunder Frank, *Crisis: in the World Economy* (Heinemann, London, 1980)

Joseph Frankel, *International Relations in a Changing World* (OUP, London, 1980)

Susan George, *How the Other Half Dies: The Real Reasons for World Hunger* (Pelican Books, Harmondsworth, 1977)

Paul Harrison, *Third World Tomorrow: A Report from the Battlefront in the War against Poverty* (Penguin, Harmondsworth, 1980)

Derek Heater, *World Studies: Education for International Understanding in Britain* (Harraps, London, 1980)

John D. Herbert, *Urban Development in the Third World: Policy Guidelines* (Praeger, New York, 1980)

Michael Kidron and Ronald Segal, *The State of the World Atlas* (Pan Books, London, 1981)

Francis Moore Lappe and Joseph Collins, *Food First: Beyond the Myth of Scarcity* (available from Centre for World Development Education, 128 Buckingham Palace Road, London SW1)

John Madeley and Geoff Tansey, *Trade – The Struggle for Partnership* (Christian Aid, One World Series, London, 1979)

David Morris, *Measuring the Condition of the World's Poor: the physical quality of life index* (Pergamon Press for the Overseas Development Council, New York, 1979)

Kathryn Morton and Peter Tulloch, *Trade and Developing Countries* (ODI and Croom Helm, 1977)

Alan Mountjoy (ed.), *The Third World: Problems and Perspectives* (Macmillan Press and The Geographical Magazine,

London, 1979)

North–South – a programme for survival: Report of the Independent Commission on International Development Issues (Pan Books, London, 1980)

Michael Noelke, *Europe–Third World Independence, Facts and Figures* (Commission of the European Communities, Development Series, 1979)

ODA, *The ABC of Aid and Development: some terms and institutions* (ODA, London, 1980)

ODA, *British Aid Statistics 1975–79* (ODA, London 1980)

Jonathan Power and Anne-Marie Holensteiner, *World of Hunger, A Strategy for Survival* (Maurice Temple Smith Ltd, London, 1976)

Hans Singer and Javed Ansari, *Rich and Poor Countries* (George Allen and Unwin, London, 1978)

World Development Report 1980 (OUP, London, 1980, for the World Bank)

The World Economic Crisis: A Commonwealth Perspective, Report by a Group of Experts (Commonwealth Secretariat, London, 1980)

Journals and Magazines

Aid and Development. Published monthly by the Centre for World Development Education

Commonwealth. Published bi-monthly by The Royal Commonwealth Society, 18 Northumberland Avenue, London WC2

Development Research Digest (twice a year) and *IDS Bulletin* (four issues a year), both available from the IDS Publications Office, Institute of Development Studies, University of Sussex, Brighton BN1 9RE

The Journal of Development Studies. Published four times a year; available from Frank Cass, Gainsborough House, 11 Gainsborough Road, London E11 1RS

Third World Quarterly. Published by the Third World Foundation, New Zealand House, 80 Haymarket, London SW1Y 4TS

South. Available from the above address

World Development. Published monthly by Pergamon Press, Headington Hill Hall, Oxford OX3 OBW

Further Information

A catalogue of literature available from many sources is issued by Third World Publications Ltd, 151 Stratford Road, Birmingham B11 1RD. The Overseas Development Institute (10–11 Percy St, London W1P OJB) produces an occasional review and also briefing papers and books.